Strengths-Based Career Development
for
School Guidance and
Counseling Programs

Norman C. Gysbers and Richard T. Lapan

Counseling Outfitters, LLC

Strengths-Based Career Development through Comprehensive Guidance and Counseling Programs

Cover photograph by Garry R. Walz, Ph.D.

We selected this photo for the cover because it reflects the myriad forces, patterns, and colors that merge together to create an attractive whole – much as career development reflects the interplay between many different influences and values.

ISBN 13: 978-0-9795668-3-7

Dedicated to R. Lynn Jensen

A career of helping students make good decisions

Strengths-Based Career Development for School Guidance and Counseling Programs

Table of Contents

Foreword

Like so many organizations in today's society, publishers are faced more than ever before with the need—no, the pressing *necessity*—to make wise choices in what they decide to publish. Galloping production costs and ever-tightening consumer budgets severely restrict a publisher's freedom to take on books that have an uncertain potential for success. Hence, fewer books can be published. Economic limitations require that a publisher judiciously select from the myriad of requests they receive to publish only those that both serve an imperative need and contain information that is of the highest quality and validity. This book meets both of these criteria.

First, the idea of the need for this book did not fall upon us like an apple out of a tree. Only after analyzing the many requests we received from school counselors, counselor educators, and other school personnel did we conclude that a real gap in the school counseling literature pertains to the career guidance component of comprehensive school guidance programs. While other components are well addressed in the literature, there has been a notable need for practical resources providing step-by-step instructions on how to implement a successful school-based career guidance program. Particularly significant has been a need to interface three emerging areas of research and development: 1) an emphasis on strengths-based counseling approaches; 2) the growing demand for counselor and program accountability; and 3) an emphasis on the importance of a seamless longitudinal development of students' skills in life/career decision making and planning. Many resources speak to the *importance* of developing such skills, but few offer specific assistance to counselors in designing and implementing successful programs to do so.

In regard to the second criterion, quality, there is no question that Norman Gysbers and Richard Lapan are eminently qualified to provide counselors with valuable insight and guidance in all three of these areas. Norm has long been a leader in the development of the comprehensive school guidance program model, the delivery of career guidance services, and the implementation of program evaluation activities. Rich has brought a fresh emphasis on students' individual career development through his conceptualization of an "Integrative/Contextual Model of Career Development" and a much needed emphasis on strengths-based career guidance.

Thus we have a relatively unattended need in school guidance and counseling programs addressed by two outstanding leaders in the guidance and counseling literature. The result is both an excellent publication and one that stands by itself in responding to a pressing need in comprehensive school guidance programs. We are assured that this book will be not only a compelling read, but a resource that counselors and counselor educators will return to again and again.

Do you like unbeatable bargains? This is one of them. We're confident that you will be constantly reassured that it serves your needs admirably well.

Garry R. Walz, Ph.D.
Jeanne C. Bleuer, Ph.D.
Counseling Outfitters, LLC

Preface

As workplaces become more global and characterized by unprecedented technological change and mobility, competition crosses international borders. Speed and innovation hold key places in competitive success; and current and future workers are learning that "business-as-usual" means integrating cultural, social, legal, political, governmental, and economic differences when creating and marketing all products and services. (Feller & Whichard, 2005, p. 23)

In this the first decade of the 21st century, Friedman (2007) declared that the "world is flat," meaning that individuals and companies are collaborating and competing globally. Why is the world flat? According to Friedman, the world is flat because of ten forces at work including the fall of the Berlin wall, the introduction of Netscape, work flow software, open-sourcing, outsourcing, offshoring, supply-chaining, insourcing, in-forming, and finally, by something he called the steroids – digital processing.

As the power of these forces continues to unfold, they are causing substantial and long lasting changes in the occupational, industrial, and social structures of the United States and countries around the world, changes that are having a dramatic impact on work, the workplace, and the lives of people. Work and workplaces are becoming more global, characterized by technological change moving at near light speed. "More and more workers and the organizations in which they work are developing global identities" (Feller & Whichard, 2005, p. 23).

Social structures and social and personal values also continue to change and become more diverse. Emerging social groups are challenging established groups, asking for equality. People are on the move, too, from rural to urban areas and back again and from one region of the country to another in search of economic, social, and psychological security. Our nation's population is becoming increasingly diverse.

All of these changes are creating substantial challenges for our children and adolescents. A rapidly changing work world and labor force in a global economy; violence in the home, school, and community; divorce; teenage suicide; substance abuse; and sexual experimentation are just a few examples. These challenges are not abstract aberrations. These challenges are real; and they are having and will have substantial impact on the career, personal/social, and academic development of our children and adolescents (Gysbers & Henderson, 2006).

Now, more than ever before, given these dramatic challenges, it is imperative that young people are prepared to make successful transitions within our educational system, to work, or to further education upon leaving our K-12 institutions, and be successful participants in the workforce. "Every student in America should graduate from high school ready for college, career, and life. Every child. No exceptions" (Gates, as cited in Alliance for Excellent Education, 2007). What knowledge, skills, and attitudes will be required of students for these purposes? The report of the New Commission on the Skills of the American Workforce (National Center on Education and the Economy, 2007) titled "Tough Choices Tough Times" recommended the following:

> Strong skills in English, mathematics, technology, and
> science, as well as literature, history, and the arts will
> be essential for many; beyond this, candidates will

have to be comfortable with ideas and abstractions, good at both analysis and synthesis, creative and innovative, self-disciplined and well organized, able to learn very quickly and work well as a member of a team and have the flexibility to adapt quickly to frequent changes in the labor market as the shifts in the economy become ever faster and more dramatic. (p. 8)

Knowledge, skills, and attitudes such as these do not appear suddenly on the day students are ready to leave school. On the contrary, they require substantial time and attention to develop, be assimilated, and used by students. They require time and attention beginning in elementary school. Their development requires strong academic and career and technical educational preparation as well as comprehensive guidance and counseling programs that feature career guidance and counseling and related academic and personal/social activities.

It is also important to remember that students are not empty vessels waiting to be filled when they come to school (Larson & Keiper, 2007). "Students come with preconceptions about how the world works which includes beliefs and prior knowledge acquired through various experiences" (Pellegrino, 2006, p. 3). Unfortunately, these preconceptions, particularly concerning the nature and structure of the world of education and work, are often incomplete, inaccurate, and stereotypical. As a result, many students begin learning about education and work in a state of educational and occupational illiteracy.

To work with students in this state, Pellegrino (2006) stressed the importance of first drawing from them what they currently know about topics such as the nature and structure of the worlds of education and work in order to build on that knowledge or to challenge it. Then, for students to develop competence in such topics, he stated they needed a foundation of factual knowledge organized within a conceptual framework that facilitates knowledge retrieval and application.

What Is This Book All About?

This book describes a conceptual framework that can provide all students K-12 with the needed factual knowledge they can retrieve and apply to successfully navigate transitions from grade to grade and to the work world or further education and then to work upon leaving school or back to education again. The conceptual framework that is used is a comprehensive guidance and counseling program (Gysbers & Henderson, 2006). A holistic strengths-based model of career development is featured that focuses career guidance and counseling and related academic and personal/social knowledge, skills, and attitudes delivered through comprehensive guidance and counseling programs. While academic knowledge and skills are critical today and will be tomorrow, they are not sufficient by themselves. Carnevale and Desrochers (2003) stated it this way:

> To be sure, everyone will need a solid academic foundation. But at some point, students will need to put an occupational [career] point on their academic pencils. (p. 228)

Part I of the book provides you with historical and theoretical foundations to give you a clear understanding of the rich history of comprehensive guidance and counseling programs in the schools. Part I also presents an integrative holistic strengths-based model of career development. Then, Part II describes comprehensive guidance and counseling programs to give you an understanding of the program framework in which career guidance and counseling is embedded and delivered.

Featured in Part II is strengths-based career development content that, when integrated into the design and application of career guidance and counseling activities, helps all students to become proactive, resilient, and adaptive adults. Also in Part II, a discussion is presented concerning the need for evidence-based activities as well as an overview of effective career guidance and counseling activities and a results-based developmental model that identifies those student outcomes likely to be impacted by such activities. In Part III, the processes used to design career guidance and counseling activities are presented along with a full discussion of the ways that career guidance and counseling activities are delivered and evaluated. This is followed by discussion of what must be done to advocate for career guidance and counseling activities within the framework of overall guidance and counseling programs.

Who Should Read This Book?

Career guidance and counseling in the schools has a long and rich history that dates back at least 100 years. During these years professional school counselors and teachers have provided students with a wide array of career guidance and counseling activities and services. These activities and services were not always provided to all students systematically and sequentially, however, because of a lack of a coherent K-12 organizational framework. Given the global economy of today and tomorrow, more must be done in our schools to engage and energize all students, helping them plan for and transition successfully into their futures. Professional school counselors, in particular, are obligated to do nothing less by their code of ethics, *Ethical Standards for School Counselors* (American School Counselor Association, 2004).

Strengths-Based Career Development for School Guidance and Counseling Programs

This book is designed for several groups of readers. The first group includes professional school counselors, teachers, administrators, and other educational personnel who have an interest in career guidance and counseling and a commitment to assisting all students K-12 acquire the knowledge, skills, and attitudes they need to make successful transitions through school and from school to work or further education and then to work. This group will find this book to be an excellent review of the theory and practice of career guidance and counseling. But, it is more than just a review for practitioners. Its three carefully crafted and connected parts follow a logical progression from historical and theoretical foundations to an organizational framework and delivery systems for career guidance and counseling to strategies for evaluating and advocating for career guidance and counseling in the schools. Thus, this book can be a source of *renewal* for practitioners. It presents a holistic strengths-based model of career development fully integrated into a comprehensive guidance and counseling program framework that provides a seamless approach to career guidance and counseling in the schools.

A second group of readers who will find this book valuable includes school counselors in training as well as other educators in training because it provides them with the necessary knowledge, skills, and attitudes to do career guidance and counseling. It offers the comprehensive guidance and counseling program framework for integrating and delivering career guidance and counseling naturally and comfortably. It also offers those in training with a perspective on the importance of career guidance and counseling for all students at all levels of K-12 education.

References

Alliance for Excellent Education. (2007, March 19). *Bill Gates testifies before Senate Committee*. Alliance For Excellent Education, *Straight A's, 7*(6), 1.

American School Counselor Association. (2004). *Ethical standards for school counselors* (2004). Alexandria, VA: Author.

Carnevale, A. P., & Desrochers, D. M. (2003). Preparing students for the knowledge economy: What school counselors need to know. *Professional School Counseling, 6*, 228-236.

Feller, R. W., & Whichard, J. (2005). *Knowledge nomads and the nervously employed: Workplace change & courageous career choices*. Austin, TX: Pro-Ed.

Friedman, T. L. (2007). *The world is flat: A brief history of the twenty-first century*. New York: Picador/Farrar, Straus and Giroux.

Gysbers, N. C., & Henderson, P. (2006). *Developing and managing your school guidance and counseling program* (4th ed.). Alexandria, VA: American Counseling Association.

Larson, B. E., & Keiper, T. A. (2007). *Instructional strategies for middle and high school*. New York: Routledge.

National Center on Education and the Economy. (2007). *Tough choices tough times: The report of the new commission on skills of the American workforce*. Washington, DC: Author.

Pellegrino, J. W. (2006). *Rethinking and redesigning curriculum, instruction and assessment: What contemporary research and theory suggests*. Washington, DC: National Center on Education and the Economy.

About the Authors

Norman C. Gysbers

Norman C. Gysbers is a Curators' Professor in the Department of Educational, School, and Counseling Psychology at the University of Missouri-Columbia. He received his B.A. degree (1954) from Hope College and his M.A. (1959) and Ph.D. (1963) degrees from the University of Michigan. He is a licensed school counselor in Missouri. He was a teacher in the public schools, a school counselor and director of guidance at the University Laboratory School, University of Missouri, and he served in the U.S. Army. He has been a visiting professor at the University of Nevada-Reno and Virginia Polytechnic Institute and State University. He was awarded a Franqui Professorship from the Universite Libre de Bruxelles, Belgium and lectured there in February, 1984. He has been a visiting scholar at the University of Hong Kong and the Chinese University of Hong Kong, and a Scholar in Residence at the University of British Columbia.

Gysbers' research and teaching interests are in career development, career counseling, and school guidance and counseling program development, management, and evaluation. He is author of 87 articles in 17 different professional journals, 33 chapters in published books, 15 monographs, and 17 books.

In 1978 he received the American Vocational Association's Division Merit Award and the Missouri Guidance Association's Outstanding Service Award. In 1981 he was awarded the National Vocational Guidance Association's

National Merit Award and in 1983 the American Counseling Association's Distinguished Professional Service Award, and the Distinguished Professional Service Award from the Missouri Association of Counselor Education and Supervision. In 1984 he received the Franqui Foundation Medal, Universite Libre de Bruxelles. In 1987 he was awarded the United States Air Force Recruiting Service's Spirit of America Award and the Distinguished Service Award of the Association of Computer-Based Systems for Career Information. In 1989 he received the National Career Development Association's Eminent Career Award and in 2000 he received the National Career Development Association's President's Recognition Award. He was awarded the American School Counselor Association Post-Secondary School Counselor of the Year Award in 2001.

Gysbers was editor of the *Career Development Quarterly,* 1962-1970; President of the National Career Development Association, 1972-73; President of the American Counseling Association, 1977-78; and Vice President of the American Vocational Association, 1979-1982. He was the editor of *The Journal of Career Development* from 1978 to 2006. Since 1967 he has served as director of numerous national and state projects on career development and career counseling, and school guidance program development, implementation, and evaluation.

Richard T. Lapan

Richard T. Lapan is a professor in and chair of the Department of Student Development and Pupil Personnel Services at the University of Massachusetts, Amherst. For the past 21 years, Dr. Lapan has taught Masters and Doctoral students in Counselor Education and Counseling Psychology. He has specialized in training Masters' level counselors to work in K16 school settings. In 1972, Dr. Lapan received his B.A. from St. Anselm's College (majoring in Philosophy). He earned his Masters' degree in 1974 from Duquesne University (Existential/ Phenomenological Counseling). In 1986, Dr. Lapan graduated with distinction from the University of Utah receiving a Ph.D. in Counseling Psychology.

Dr. Lapan has had extensive experience providing counseling services (career, family, individual, group, and residential) to children, adolescents, and adults. From 1975 until 1980, Dr. Lapan worked as a Masters' level counselor providing counseling, educational, and residential treatment services for urban, suburban, and rural adolescents in Massachusetts. He has worked in several school settings and psychiatric hospitals. After completing his doctorate, Dr. Lapan provided career counseling services to adults who were in the process of making significant career and life changes.

Dr. Lapan's research applies a scientist-practitioner model to the project of providing effective counseling services to children, adolescents, and young adults. He has published numerous articles and presented these research findings at many national conferences. He was editor of *Professional School Counseling*, 2003-2006. Dr. Lapan has received several federal and state grants to fund his research.

In 2000, Dr. Lapan received the Distinguished Service Award from the Guidance Division of the Association for Career and Technical Education, and in 2006, he received the Counselor Educator of the Year Award from the American School Counselor Association. His research work focuses on developing empirically supported development and prevention programs. This professional emphasis has led to a commitment to improve the lives of young people in our society through the implementation of research enhanced, comprehensive school counseling programs.

Acknowledgements

Several years ago, Dr. Garry Walz asked us to consider writing a book that emphasized career development and career guidance within the framework of comprehensive guidance and counseling programs. We were delighted to accept the invitation because we too wanted to show and stress the importance of a holistic view of career development as being a vital part of comprehensive guidance and counseling programs. We are very pleased with our working relationship with Counseling Outfitters, LLC; and wish to express our thanks to Garry and Dr. Jeanne Bleuer for their encouragement and very able assistance throughout the writing process.

We also want to acknowledge and give special thanks to Linda Coats for her invaluable assistance in helping prepare this book for publication.

Part I.
Historical and Theoretical Foundations

Chapter 1

The Evolution of Career Guidance and Counseling in the Schools

Guidance and counseling in the schools began as vocational guidance at the beginning of the 1900s. Through the decades that followed, educational guidance and personal/social guidance were added to vocational guidance as processes to assist individuals make educational decisions and deal with personal/social concerns. Vocational guidance remained over these same decades, continuing to focus on helping individuals make occupational choices and transitions from school to work and further education.

The 1940s and 1950s witnessed the beginning of theory building to undergird the practice of vocational guidance. During this time period, the word *career* gradually began to replace the word *vocational* in the literature. Also, the word *development* was added to the word *career* to describe a process over time. Career theory development to undergird career guidance and counseling (as we call it today) continues unabated today as new theoretical perspectives continue to emerge in the literature (Niles & Harris-Bowlsbey, 2005).

While work on the theory and practice of vocational guidance was taking place in the 1900s, work was also underway as to how best to conceptualize, organize, administer, and evaluate the practice of vocational guidance in the schools. As the 1900s began to unfold, vocational guidance first became institutionalized and practiced as a position. Then in the 1920s and 1930s, educational and personal/social guidance were added to vocational guidance to more adequately meet the needs of all students. In the 1930s, the resulting combination of the three types of guidance and the position of school counselor were embedded in an organizational structure called guidance services, which, in turn, was placed in a broader structure called pupil personnel services.

Later, in the 1970s and 1980s, the position and services conceptualizations of guidance along with the three types of guidance were incorporated into the comprehensive program approach to guidance in the schools. Within the program conceptualization, career guidance and counseling remains a major priority today. Comprehensive guidance and counseling programs in the schools have had and will continue to have a career profile.

Chapter 1 tells the story of the evolution of the practice of vocational guidance to the theory of career development and the practice of career guidance and counseling. The Chapter also describes how guidance and counseling evolved in the schools, first as a position focusing on vocational guidance, to a service emphasizing vocational (career) guidance, personal/social guidance, and educational guidance, to a comprehensive program that fully integrates these three types of guidance. Special attention is given to the important and central roles that career development concepts and career guidance and counseling practices had and continue to have on these programs in elementary, middle, and high schools.

In the Beginning: A Focus on Vocational Guidance

Guidance and counseling were born during the height of the Progressive Movement as "but one manifestation of the broader movement of progressive reform which occurred in this country in the late 19th and early 20th centuries" (Stephens, 1970, p. 5). The beginnings of guidance and counseling can be traced to the work of a number of individuals and social institutions. People such as Charles Merrill, Frank Parsons, Meyer Bloomfield, Jessie Davis, Anna Reed, E. W. Weaver, and David Hill, working through a number of organizations and movements such as the settlement house movement, the National Society for the Promotion of Industrial Education, and schools in San Francisco, Detroit, Grand Rapids, Seattle, New York, and New Orleans, were all instrumental in formulating and implementing early conceptions of guidance and counseling.

During these early years, guidance and counseling was called vocational guidance. The term was first used by Parsons in 1908 to describe an organized service consisting of a scientific approach to choosing a vocation (Davis, 1914).

> No step in life, unless it may be the choice of a husband or wife, is more important than the choice of a vocation. The wise selection of the business, profession, trade, or occupation to which one's life is to be devoted and the development of full efficiency in the chosen field are matters of deepest movement to young men and to the public. These vital problems should be solved in a careful, scientific way, with due regard to each person's aptitudes, abilities, ambitions resources, and limitations, and the relations of these elements to the conditions of success in different industries. (Parsons, 1909, p. 3)

It is important to note that Parsons (1909) used the term vocational guidance to describe an organized service. In doing so he described a process to assist individuals to make the transition from school to work by choosing a vocation.

> Yet there is no part of life where the need for guidance is more emphatic than in the transition from school to work – the choice of a vocation, adequate preparation for it, and the attainment of efficiency and success. The building of a career is quite as difficult a problem as the building of a house, yet few ever sit down with pencil and paper, with expert information and counsel, to plan a working career and deal with the life problem scientifically, as they would deal with the problem of building a house, taking the advice of an architect to help them. (Parsons, 1909, p. 4)

This is an interesting statement because Parsons (1909) uses the terms "vocation" and "career" in the same paragraph. Later in his book, Parsons uses the terms "working career" (p. 98), "scientific choice of occupation" (p. 99), "building up a successful career" (p. 100), and "building a career" (p. 101). It is unclear as to the meanings Parsons attached to the words "vocation," "career," and "occupation" in these contexts. It appears that he used them to mean the same thing. Whatever his meanings, however, one could read into his usage of the terms a glimmer of the broader meaning of career and the notion of career development that was to unfold later, beginning in the 1950s and 60s.

In the next decade of the 1900s, the meaning of vocational guidance broadened to include educational and social concerns.

Vocational guidance was seen as a response to the economic, educational, and social problems of those times and was concerned about the entrance of young people into the work world and the conditions they might find there. Economic concerns focused on the need to better prepare workers for the workplace, whereas educational concerns arose from a need to increase efforts in schools to help students find purpose for their education as well as their employment. Social concerns emphasized the need for changing school methods and organization as well as exerting more control over conditions of labor in child-employing industries (U.S. Bureau of Education, 1914).

The Position of Vocational Counselor

The work of Frank Parsons and the Vocation Bureau soon became known across the country. Out of it grew the first National Conference on Vocational Guidance, held in Boston in 1910, followed by a similar conference in New York in 1912 and the formation of the National Vocational Guidance Association in Grand Rapids in 1913 (Ryan, 1919). It also had a direct impact on the Boston public schools because in 1909 the Boston School Committee asked personnel in the Vocation Bureau to outline a program of vocational guidance for the public schools of Boston. On June 7, 1909, the Boston School Committee approved the bureau's suggestion and "instructed the Superintendent of Schools to appoint a committee of six to work with the director" (Bloomfield, 1915, p. 34). Upon completion of its work, the committee issued a report that identified three primary aims for vocational guidance in the Boston schools:

> Three aims have stood out above all others: first, to secure thoughtful consideration, on the part of parents, pupils, and teachers, of the importance of

> a life-career motive; second, to assist in every way possible in placing pupils in some remunerative work on leaving school; and third, to keep in touch with and help them thereafter, suggesting means of improvement and watching the advancement of those who need such aid. (Bloomfield, 1915, p. 36)

These aims were implemented by a central office staff and by appointed vocational counselors in each elementary and secondary school in Boston. Teachers were appointed to the position of vocational counselor often with no relief from their teaching duties and with no additional pay (Brewer, 1922; Ginn, 1924). The vocational counseling duties these teachers were asked to perform were in addition to their regular teaching duties.

New Types of Guidance

The 1920s witnessed the continued expansion of guidance and counseling in the schools. During this period of time, the nature and structure of guidance and counseling were being influenced by the mental hygiene and measurement movements, developmental studies of children, the introduction of cumulative records, and progressive education. In effect, "Vocational guidance was taking on the new vocabulary present in the culture at large and in the educational subculture; the language of mental health, progressive education, child development, and measurement theory" (Johnson, 1972, p. 160).

As a result of these influences there was less emphasis on guidance for vocation (vocational guidance) and more on education as guidance (educational guidance). This shift in emphasis in the purpose of guidance occurred partly because of newer leadership, particularly on the part of people such as John

Brewer, who were more educationally oriented. In the late teens, Brewer (1918) defined educational guidance "as a conscious effort to assist in the intellectual growth of an individual. …Anything that has to do with instruction or with learning may come under the term educational guidance" (p. 14). According to Myers (1935), this view of educational guidance "practically identifies educational guidance with organized education" (p. 7).

In the 1930s, as a result of the mental health movement, a clinical model of guidance focusing on personal/social issues began to dominate professional theory and practice. Rudy (1965) stressed this point when he stated:

> Up to 1930…not much progress had been made in differentiating this function [personal counseling] from the preexisting programs of vocational and educational guidance. After that date, more and more of a separation appeared as guidance workers in the high schools became aware of increasingly large numbers of students who were troubled by personal problems involving hostility to authority, sex relationships, unfortunate home situations, and financial stringencies. (p. 25)

Increasingly too, the term guidance was seen as an all-inclusive term focusing on "problems of adjustment to health, religion, recreation, to family and friends, to school and to work" (Campbell, 1932, p. 4). Vocational guidance remained, but it continued to be defined more narrowly as occupational choice, preparing for it, entering into it, and progressing in it.

> Vocational guidance is the process of assisting the individual to choose an occupation, prepare for it,

enter upon and progress in it. It is concerned primarily with helping individuals make decisions and choices involved in planning a future and building a career—decisions and choices necessary in effecting satisfactory vocational adjustment. (Myers, 1941, p. 3)

The 1930s also showed an emphasis on education as guidance. Efforts were made by some to interpret much, if not all, of education as guidance. Miller (1961), somewhat sarcastically noted that "through the 1930s guidance was in danger of being so absorbed into curriculum revision, in particular and into the educational effort in general, that even a congressional investigating committee would not be able to recognize it as a function existing in its own right" (p. 6). At the same time, personal counseling, with its emphasis on personal adjustment, continued to be emphasized as well.

While the emphasis on personal/social guidance continued in the 1940s, vocational guidance also showed strength. This was evident in provisions of the Vocational Education Act of 1946. It provided funds for a federal office and for state support for vocational guidance in the schools. Then, a major piece of federal legislation in the 1950s that was to have substantial impact on how the purpose of guidance in the schools was framed was the National Defense Education Act of 1958. The purpose of guidance according to this act was the "identification and counseling of scientifically talented students" (Herr, 2001, p. 238). Educational guidance became a priority.

A New Organizational Structure for Guidance and Counseling

During the 1920s and 1930s, while educational guidance and personal/social guidance were added to vocational guidance as additional types, the organizational structure for guidance in the schools also was undergoing change. What had been a position (a vocational counselor with a list of duties) was evolving to become a position in a defined grouping of guidance services, which in turn were embedded in a larger organizational framework called pupil personnel services. Five or more services for guidance were identified including individual inventory, occupational and educational information, counseling, placement, follow-up, and sometimes orientation. According to Roeber, Walz, and Smith (1969):

> This conception of guidance services was developed during a period in the history of the guidance movement when it was necessary to have some definitive statement regarding the need for and nature of a more organized form of guidance. This delineating of guidance services generally served its purpose and gave the guidance movement something tangible to "sell" to state departments of education and to local schools. (p. 55)

Career Theory Building Begins

In their book *Occupational Choice*, Ginzberg, Ginsburg, Axelrod, and Herma (1951) stated that vocational counselors counseled without theory to guide them. Vocational guidance was a process without a base in theory.

> Vocational counselors are busy practitioners anxious to improve their counseling techniques. They are constantly on the lookout for helpful tools, and the research-minded among them devote what time they can to devising better techniques. They are not theoreticians working on the problem of how individuals make their occupational choices, for, though they have no bias against theory, they have had little time to invest in developing one. (p. 7)

Ginzberg et al. responded by proposing a theory of occupational choice they suggested extended over a period of ten years. Later, Super (1953) presented a life long view of career development in ten propositions that summarized a comprehensive theory. Roe (1956) followed, describing her view concerning career development in her book *The Psychology of Occupations*. Then Holland (1959) presented his theory of vocational choice "in terms of the occupational environments, the person and his (sic) development, and the interactions of the person and the vocational environment" (p. 35).

Vocational Guidance or Career Guidance?

During the 1960s and 1970s, knowledge of human development in occupational, vocational, and career terms increased dramatically. Increasingly, the term "career" became more popular as a way of describing this knowledge. In 1966, the National Vocational Guidance Association undertook a study of the nature and status of contemporary vocational guidance. It was called Project Reconceptualization. Papers were prepared by Field (1966), Katz (1966), and Super (1966). One of the questions asked was "Should the term be vocational guidance or career guidance?" While a definitive answer was not forthcoming to this question in these papers and the discussions that followed, the fact that Project Reconceptualization was initiated and the question was asked, indicated that changes were underway.

In 1973, the National Vocational Guidance Association (NVGA) published a position paper (done jointly with the American Vocational Association) that defined career and career development. In essence, it defined career as "a time-extended working out of a purposeful life pattern through work undertaken by the individual" (National Vocational Guidance Association, 1973, p. 7). Career development was defined as "the total constellation of psychological, sociological, educational, physical, economic, and chance factors that combine to shape the career of any given individual" (p. 7).

Before the NVGA position statement was presented in the above document, there was discussion of a variety of perspectives of career. At the one extreme, some people equated occupation and career while, at the other extreme, career was describe as a general life pattern that included virtually all activities. Then it was pointed out that some writers delimited this broad definition somewhat by focusing on the major life domains which engage the individual in multiple roles (e.g., worker, family member, community participant and leisure-time participant).

The expanded view of the career concept as embodied in the NVGA position statement broke the time barrier that previously restricted the vision of career to only a cross-sectional view of an individual's life. As Super and Bohn (1970, p. 115) pointed out, "it is well . . . to keep clear the distinction between occupation (what one does) and career (the course pursued over a period to time)." It was more appropriate, too, because the career concept has become the basis for organizing and interpreting the impact that the role of work has on individuals over their lifetimes. Past, present, and possible future work (occupational) and related behaviors can be understood in the context of an individual's overall development. Thus, the expanded view of career placed emphasis on "vocational histories rather than on status at a single point in time, on career criteria rather than occupational criteria" (Jordaan, 1974, p. 264).

Guidance and Counseling Reconceptualized as a Program

By the late 1960s, it became apparent that the traditional formulations of guidance—the position, the six guidance services (orientation, information, assessment, counseling, placement and follow-up) and the three types of guidance (educational, personal/social, and vocational) were no longer adequate formulations. The position within the guidance services model was often seen as ancillary or supportive to curriculum and instruction, not equal and complementary. The three types of guidance resulted frequently in fragmented and event oriented activities, and, in some instances, the development of separate kinds of guidance programs and counselors. Educational guidance was stressed by academic/college personnel, personal-social guidance became the territory of mental health workers, and vocational guidance became the focus of labor economists and career and technical education personnel.

To meet the needs of students and their parents, what was needed was an organized program of guidance and counseling, a program that was equal and complementary with other programs in education. What was needed was an organizational structure in the schools that could provide and support a developmental program for all students that would feature content for guidance, individual planning for students, and counseling, consultation, and referral, as well as program management and consultative services that supported other programs in the schools. What emerged was the comprehensive guidance and counseling program that incorporated the position and services models (American School Counselor Association, 2005; Gysbers & Henderson, 2006; Johnson & Johnson, 2001; Myrick, 2003).

As the decades of the 1950s, 1970s, 1980s, and 1990s unfolded, guidance and counseling in the schools, now becoming a comprehensive program, continued to respond to national needs and concerns. Social problems including substance abuse, violence in the schools, mental health issues, and changing family patterns, all pulled and tugged at defining the purpose of guidance and counseling in the schools and the role of school counselors. At the same time, economic issues dealing with changing labor force needs and globalization of industry were also present. The changing labor force and globalization of industry renewed interest in vocational guidance (now called career guidance) as expressed in federal vocational education legislation, the Vocational Education Act of 1963, the Carl D. Perkins Vocational Education Act of 1984, the Carl D. Perkins Vocational Education and Applied Technology Education Act Amendments of 1990, the Carl D. Perkins Vocational-Technical Education Act Amendments of 1998, and the Carl D. Perkins Career and Technical Education Improvement Act of 2006.

The Current Status of Career Guidance and Counseling

Even though educational guidance (today the word academic is used more frequently) and personal/social guidance were more prominent at various times during the decades of the 1900s, career guidance and counseling has always had a strong presence in school guidance. Why? Because the needs of the United States have always required career guidance and counseling in schools (Carnevale & Desrochers, 2003; Feller, 2003). This is evident by how career guidance and counseling has been supported by federal legislation since the 1940s. It is also evident by the language embodied in the Association for Career and Technical Education (2003) position paper supporting comprehensive school guidance programs that have a strong focus on career development and career interventions in schools.

Today, in the United States, the major way to organize guidance and counseling activities and services in schools is the comprehensive guidance program (American School Counselor Association, 2005; Gysbers & Henderson, 2006; Johnson & Johnson, 2001; Myrick, 2003). The use of the comprehensive guidance program approach began as early as the 1980s (Gysbers & Moore, 1981), based on work undertaken in the 1970s (Gysbers & Moore, 1974). The American School Counselor Association (ASCA) endorsed the concept by publishing the ASCA National Model (ASCA, 2005).

A comprehensive guidance and counseling program as described by Gysbers and Henderson (2006) consists of four elements; content, organizational framework, resources, and development, management, and accountability. The content element contains knowledge and skills (cast as standards) considered important for students to acquire as a result of their participation in a school district's comprehensive guidance and counseling program. The organizational framework contains three structural components (definition, rationale, assumptions), four program components (guidance curriculum, individual student planning, responsive services, system support), along with a suggested distribution of school counselor time by grade levels across the four program components. The resource element consists of the human, financial, and political resources required to fully implement the program. Finally, the development, management, and accountability element describes the five transition phases required to fully operationalize a comprehensive guidance and counseling program along with the management tasks involved as well as the three types of accountability: program, personnel, and results.

Career guidance and counseling standards, activities, and services are embedded in comprehensive guidance and counseling programs in at least four ways. First, the content elements of all state and local school district programs contain career development guidance standards for students to master. Second, the guidance curriculum component features career guidance and counseling activities in which all students participate in order for them to acquire the needed career development competence. Third, the individual student planning component contains activities to help all students develop individual life career plans, sometimes called personal plans, for progress or personal plans of study. And finally, fourth, the responsive services component offers individual and small group counseling to students who may require more in depth assistance as they consider their next steps educationally and occupationally.

Looking Ahead: The Importance of Career Guidance and Counseling

The new economy with its emphasis on globalization, downsizing, flexibility, and constant change is a reality that affects the social, economic, and educational systems. Social system change can be seen in generational differences and the altering of family configurations. Economic systems involve ideas of equality and inequity, with the need to balance disparities of income, wage fluctuations, and changing governmental involvement. Educational systems are affected by the need to train students to deal with work and life in the future, which can involve new configurations of programs to allow for differences in training for various career options, with an emphasis on developing the creativity and flexibility that will be needed for the workplace of the future. (Peterson & Gonzalez, 2005, p. 40)

While career guidance and counseling has always occupied an important role and place in guidance and counseling since the turn of the last century, it has assumed an even more prominent role and place in guidance and counseling in the schools today. One reason is the rapidly changing nature and structure of the work world brought on by technology and globalization as described by Peterson and Gonzalez (2005). Another reason is that guidance and counseling in the schools has moved from a position-services model to a comprehensive program in which career guidance and counseling content is mandated and delivered regularly and systematically through the guidance curriculum, individual student planning, and responsive services.

In the chapters that follow, an integrative conceptual theory of career development is described that provides a foundation for and a source of career guidance and counseling content and activities (Lapan, 2004). Then, attention is given to a description of comprehensive guidance and counseling programs that provide an organizational framework in which to place and deliver career guidance and counseling activities. Next, example evidence-based career guidance and counseling activities for use in elementary, middle, and high schools are presented followed by an examination of how to design and deliver career guidance and counseling activities K-12 using the organizational framework of comprehensive guidance and counseling programs. Finally, how to evaluate career guidance and counseling activities and the importance of advocating for career guidance and counseling as an integral part of comprehensive guidance and counseling are highlighted.

References

American School Counselor Association. (2005). *The ASCA national model: A framework for school counseling programs* (2nd ed.). Alexandria, VA: Author.

Association for Career and Technical Education. (2003). *The role of the guidance profession in a shifting education system.* Alexandria, VA: Author.

Bloomfield, M. (1915). *Youth, school and vocation.* Boston: Houghton Mifflin Company.

Brewer, J. M. (1918). *The vocational guidance movement.* New York: Macmillan.

Brewer, J. M. (1922). *The vocational-guidance movement.* New York: Macmillan.

Campbell, M. E. (1932). *Vocational guidance committee on vocational guidance and child labor Section III Education and training* (White House Conference on Child Health and Protection). New York: Century.

Carl D. Perkins Career and Technical Education Improvement Act of 2006, Pub. L, No. 109-270.

Carl D. Perkins Vocational Education Act of 1984, Pub. L, No. 98-524, Part 1, Stat. 2433 (1984).

Carl D. Perkins Vocational Education and Applied Technology Education Act Amendments of 1990, Pub. L, No. 101-392, Part 2, Stat. 753 (1990).

Carl D. Perkins Vocational-Technical Education Act Amendments of 1998, Pub. L, No. 105-332, 112, Part 1, Stat. 3076 (1998).

Carnevale, A. P., & Desrochers, D. M. (2003). Preparing students for the knowledge economy: What school counselors need to know. *Professional School Counseling, 6*, 228-236.

Davis, J. B. (1914). *Vocational and moral guidance.* Boston: Ginn.

Feller, R. W. (2003). Aligning school counseling, the changing workplace, and career development assumptions. *Professional School Counseling, 6*, 262-271.

Field, F. L. (1966). *A taxonomy of educational processes, the nature of vocational guidance, and some implications for professional preparation.* Unpublished manuscript.

Ginn, S. J. (1924). Vocational guidance in Boston public schools. *The Vocational Guidance Magazine, 3*, 3-7.

Ginzberg, E., Ginsburg, S. W., Axelrod, S., & Herma, J. L. (1951). *Occupational choice: An approach to a general theory.* New York: Columbia University Press.

Gysbers, N. C., & Henderson, P. (2006). *Developing and managing your school guidance and counseling program* (4th ed.). Alexandria, VA: American Counseling Association.

Gysbers, N. C., & Moore, E. J. (1974). *Career guidance, counseling, and placement: elements of an illustrative program guide.* Columbia, MO: University of Missouri.

Gysbers, N. C., & Moore, E. J. (1981). *Improving guidance programs.* Englewood Cliffs, NJ: Prentice-Hall.

Herr, E. L. (2001). The impact of national policies, economics, and school reform on comprehensive guidance programs. *Professional School Counseling, 4*, 236-245.

Holland, J. L. (1959). A theory of vocational choice. *Journal of Counseling Psychology, 6*, 35-45.

Johnson, A. H. (1972). Changing conceptions of vocational guidance and concomitant value-orientations 1920-30. *Dissertation Abstracts International, 33*, 3292A (UMI No. 72-31, 933).

Johnson, C. D., & Johnson, S. K. (2001). *Results-based student support programs: Leadership academy workbook.* San Juan Capistrano, CA: Professional Update.

Jordaan, J. P. (1974). Life stages as organizing modes of career development. In E. L. Herr (Ed.), *Vocational guidance and human development* (pp. 263-295). Boston: Houghton Mifflin.

Katz, M. (1966). *The name and nature of vocational guidance.* Unpublished manuscript.

Lapan, R. T. (2004). *Career development across the K-16 years.* Alexandria, VA: American Counseling Association.

Miller, C. H. (1961). *Foundations of guidance.* New York: Harper Row.

Myers, G. E. (1935). *Relations between vocational guidance and educational guidance.* Ann Arbor, MI: The Vocational Education Department, University of Michigan.

Myers, G. E. (1941). *Principles and techniques of vocational guidance.* New York: McGraw-Hill.

Myrick, R. D. (2003). *Developmental guidance and counseling: A practical approach* (4th ed.). Minneapolis, MN: Educational Media Corporation.

National Defense Education Act of 1958, Pub. L. No. 85-864, 70, Part 1, Stat. 1580-1605 (1959).

National Vocational Guidance Association. (1973). *Position paper on career development.* Washington, DC: Author.

Niles, S. G., & Harris-Bowlsbey, J. (2005). *Career development interventions in the 21st century* (2nd ed.). Upper Saddle River, NJ: Pearson.

Parsons, F. (1909). *Choosing a vocation.* Boston: Houghton Mifflin.

Peterson, N., & Gonzalez, R. C. (2005). *The role of work in people's lives* (2nd ed.). Belmont, CA: Thomson Brooks/Cole.

Roe, A. (1956). *The psychology of occupations.* New York: John Wiley & Sons.

Roeber, E. C., Walz, G. R., & Smith, G. E. (1969). *A strategy for guidance.* New York: Macmillan.

Rudy, W. S. (1965). *Schools in an age of mass culture.* Englewood Cliffs, NJ: Prentice-Hall.

Ryan, W. C., Jr. (1919). *Vocational guidance and the public schools* (Bulletin 1918, No. 24). Washington, DC: U.S. Department of the Interior, Bureau of Education.

Stephens, W. R. (1970). *Social reform and the origins of vocational guidance.* Washington, DC: National Vocational Guidance Association.

Super, D. E. (1953). A theory of vocational development. *American Psychologist, 30,* 185-190.

Super, D. E. (1966). *A reconceptualization of vocational guidance.* Unpublished manuscript.

Super, D. E., & Bohn, M. J., Jr. (1970). *Occupational psychology.* Belmont, CA: Wadsworth Publishing Company.

United States Bureau of Education (1914). *Vocational guidance.* Papers presented at the organization meeting of the Vocational Guidance Association, Grand Rapids, Michigan, October 21-24, 1913. Prefatory Statement (Bulletin, 1914, No. 14, Whole Number 587). Washington, DC: U.S. Government Printing Office.

Vocational Education Act of 1946, Pub. L. No. 79-586, 60, Part 1, Stat. 775-778 (1947).

Vocational Education Act of 1963, Pub., L. No. 88-210, 77, Stat. 403 (1963).

Chapter 2

**The Integrative Contextual Theory of Career Development:
A Strengths-Based Model to Guide Your Work**

In the late 1990s, efforts were undertaken to evaluate the impact of community career partnerships that had been funded by the School-to-Work Opportunities Act of 1994. In one study, the directors responsible for implementing and evaluating local and regional partnerships were interviewed (Lapan, Osana, Tucker, & Kosciulek, 2002). While their commitment and efforts to help their students were very impressive, there was a glaring absence of a theoretical model or a developmental understanding of the person that these highly capable professionals could use to guide their intervention and evaluation work. Program coordinators could voice that they wanted good things for their students, like making better transitions from high school to postsecondary training; but not one coordinator could articulate an overall framework that would help to identify, organize, and evaluate the essential formative and summative outcomes that the program was trying to achieve. There was no evidence of a well-articulated career model of the developing young person that would assist these directors to understand what strengths these students needed to develop if they were going to reach the goals outlined in the federal legislation.

To address this dilemma, several questions needed to be both asked and answered. For example, in a pluralistic democracy, competing in a global marketplace, and riding on the wave of incredible technological innovation:

- What kind of a strengths-based engagement in the present and orientation to the future do we want all young people to develop before they graduate from high school?
- What kinds of strengths-based interaction patterns in the present and approaches to possible future career selves will provide a base that will nourish children and adolescents both now and across their life spans?
- By the time adolescents graduate from high school, what strengths do they need to have integrated into their everyday style of managing present tasks and settings (e.g., school); and how should they be approaching their futures (e.g., postsecondary options)?

Fortunately, the existing career development literature provides some guidelines and initial answers to these questions. For example, Super (1954) had already been grappling with these issues when he outlined what effective career counseling services would look like. He argued that research was needed to identify the "traits and trends of development observed in adolescence" (p. 18) that lead young people to more successful vocational patterns in adulthood.

To answer our questions and develop a model supported by empirical research that professional school counselors, teachers, school administrators, and theorists could apply to their work, we developed a theoretical model that synthesized many of the leading ideas in the career development literature (Lapan, 2004). This chapter presents this integrative contextual model of career development and describes the strengths-based aspects of human growth that all young people need to master before they graduate from high school. First, we present the theory. Then we describe fully the strength-based constructs central to young peoples' career development. Finally, we provide a discussion that links this model to the need to develop, implement, and evaluate career guidance and counseling interventions being provided through comprehensive guidance and counseling programs.

The Integrative Contextual Model of Career Development

Figure 2-1 presents *The Integrative Contextual Model of Career Development* (Lapan, 2004) and illustrates its four major parts. First, and at the center of our work, is the need to help all young people develop a proactive, resilient, and adaptive orientation to the present and the future. Second is a set of six strength-based constructs that contribute to either growth or lack of development of this style of engaging the world. Third is an interwoven network of cultural, economic, historical, demographic, and political contexts that shape, nurture, ignore, or impair these six strength-based constructs. Fourth is a set of critical formative and summative outcomes related to the development of these six strength-based constructs that occur across the K-16 years that significantly increase the chances that a young person will find success and satisfaction in adulthood. Brief descriptions of each of these four parts are provided below.

In answer to the question of the kinds of engagement in the present and orientation to the future that we want all young people to develop before they graduate from high school, many career theorists would argue that young people need to develop a proactive, resilient, and adaptive style of interacting in the present and use that style to assertively move towards self-defined career futures that add meaning, purpose, and satisfaction to their lives (e.g., Blustein, 2006; Claes & Ruiz-Quintanilla, 1998; Lapan, 2007; Richardson, 1998; and Savickas, 1997). Adolescents need

Strengths-Based Career Development for School Guidance and Counseling Programs

Figure 2-1

The Integrative/Contextual Model of Career development

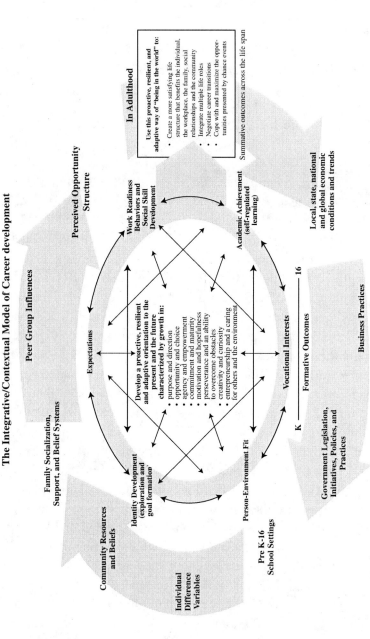

Note: From *Career development across the K–16 years: Connecting the present to satisfying and successful futures,* by R. T. Lapan, 2004, Alexandria, VA: American Counseling Association. Copyright 2004 by the American Counseling Association. Reprinted with permission.

to: engage in critical life contexts (e.g., school and community) with purpose and direction; respond to opportunities and make good decisions; act with personal agency and empowerment; exhibit a mature commitment to a self-defined direction; feel hopeful, motivated, and optimistic about their lives; be able to persevere to overcome obstacles and turn unexpected events into positive opportunities; be creative and curious; and be able to balance entrepreneurial skills and motives with concern for others and the fragile ecosystems that we need to survive. Adolescents who act with a greater sense of direction, maturity, hopefulness, empowerment, perseverance, creativity, entrepreneurship, and have intimate and caring relationships with others will be both more successful and more satisfied. Internalizing these attributes into how they go about routinely engaging in important life contexts will provide these young people adaptive advantages across their life spans.

The question we must ask is how can career guidance and counseling activities and interventions delivered through comprehensive guidance and counseling programs help young people to regularly employ such a proactive, resilient, and adaptive orientation? The answer is by helping young people more fully develop and internalize six key strength-based constructs. Career theorists and researchers have long argued that this more optimal approach to engaging in the present and moving towards desired futures is made possible if young people: (a) believe in themselves by holding positive efficacy expectation and performance enhancing attributions (Lent, Brown, & Hackett, 1994; Weiner, 1986); (b) create a self-defined identity through the interrelated processes of exploration and goal formation (Flum & Blustein, 2000); (c) develop a more complete understanding of themselves, the world of work, and how to match this self-knowledge to valued career options (Holland,

1997; Parsons, 1909); (d) pursue their intrinsic interests (Strong, 1927, 1943); (e) achieve academically and become a self-regulated and lifelong learner (Zimmerman & Schunk, 2001); and (f) employ a complex set of social skills, pro-social skills, and work-readiness behaviors (Bloch, 1996).

The double-headed arrows in Figure 2-1 point to the fact that these strength-based constructs are not independent from each other, but in fact are in dynamic interaction with each other. Unfortunately, too many career theories emphasize one or two constructs to the exclusion of the others. One result of this is the often-found failure of popular theories to adequately predict outcomes (e.g., career success and satisfaction) that follow from basic assumptions and hypotheses of their model (see, for example, Spokane's 1985 review or Tranberg, Slane, & Ekeberg, 1993). A more comprehensive model is needed that integrates the range of critical constructs that play significant roles in the journey towards career success and satisfaction. These constructs do not act alone, but interact with each other and the powerful contexts that shape them.

For example, imagine a 17-year old high school junior. She doesn't like what she is learning in school and gets low grades. Her professional school counselor arranges for her to participate in a job-shadowing experience in the district's laser technology program that is offered through their career technical high school. After actively exploring this environment, she likes what she sees and is motivated to establish a goal of attending this program. Heightened interest in what she is learning could encourage her to exhibit more cooperative social skills and to be on time, attentive, and more diligent in her work (critical work-readiness behaviors). Improving grades serve as a mastery experience that increases her self-efficacy expectations. Throughout this process, this young woman's understanding of herself in relation to the world of work is altered as she strives to reach a new agreement between newly perceived options and academic successes in contrast to how she may have understood herself and envisioned her future before this new learning experience.

The six constructs work together to promote her newfound success and define a new sense of purpose and direction in her life, as well as liberating her creativity, curiosity, and passion. As she feels more committed to a direction, each of the six constructs can themselves be changed (e.g., goals can become more detailed, complex, and well laid out as she plans for the next steps of her life's career journey). This adolescent begins to see before herself the opportunity for choice, purpose, meaning, a willingness to strive to overcome obstacles, and a strong motivation to pursue a desired future. These strength-based constructs work together to shape the career development journey and academic achievement for all of our young people. Career interventions should focus on enhancing these constructs in the lives of all students before they graduate from high school.

Strengths-based career development takes place on a stage that is designed and managed by an all-pervasive web of social, cultural, demographic, economic, historical, and political contexts. Figure 2-1 identifies on the outside of the circle some of the major contexts that career guidance and counseling efforts need to address. These contexts create the "cafeteria of experiences" that encourage or discourage young people from developing certain kinds of strengths, talents, and interests, and ultimately pursuing or ruling out a wide range of potentially satisfying career pathways (Lykken, Bouchard, McGue, & Tellegen, 1993). Young people learn and integrate our six key strength-based career development constructs in environments permeated with the influence of these powerful and often unseen forces (e.g., socioeconomic, racial, and gendered social contexts). For example, K-12 students come to have confidence in their ability to pursue certain career pathways (e.g., math and science) if their school, family, and community contexts work together to support the development of this self-understanding. Enhanced self-efficacy expectations that empower young people to see choices before them, persevere through the challenges to reach these desired options, and be hopeful about their futures are nurtured or not encouraged to develop by these surrounding contexts. Career guidance and counseling interventions must be very intentional in addressing these forces and building scaffolds of support that bridge a young person's present to desired possible career selves (Markus & Nurius, 1986) when these background contexts work against the optimal growth of our students.

Finally, Figure 2-1 points out that the development of these six strength-based constructs and resulting qualities of a proactive style of engaging the world to a great extent shape the transition process to young adulthood for our students. The development that we can help them to internalize before they graduate from high school has real consequence for their future lives. Career guidance and counseling efforts can help young people develop more satisfying life structures in adulthood (Super, Savickas, & Super, 1996), successfully integrate multiple life roles into affirming life patterns (Gysbers, Heppner, & Johnston, 2009), negotiate inevitable career transitions (Schlossberg, Waters, & Goodman, 1995), and take full advantage of the career opportunities provided by chance events (Mitchell, Levin, & Krumboltz, 1999). During the K-12 years, developmental career counseling initiatives have a central role to play in determining the kinds of summative outcomes young people realize across their life spans. These are not ancillary services. Career guidance and counseling activities delivered through comprehensive guidance and counseling programs are located at the heart of every effective school system.

Six Critical Strength-Based Constructs

The following paragraphs describe each of the six critical strength-based constructs for optimal career development across the K-12 years. Career guidance and counseling activities and services should be focused to assist all students to learn and internalize these attitudes, skills, and behavioral styles. A more complete discussion of each construct can be found in Lapan (2004, 2007).

Positive Expectations. To create meaning and exercise control over our lives, human beings employ a range of cognitive self-regulatory processes (Bandura, 1997). Self-efficacy expectations and optimistic attributional styles have been found to be key players in promoting the kinds of formative and summative outcomes career guidance and counseling services seek to enhance (Lent et al., 1994, 2000; Luzzo & Jenkins Smith, 1998). Social Cognitive Career Theory (Lent et al.) is an attempt to understand career development from the enormous research base that supports the influence of self-efficacy expectations on human behavior across diverse domains (e.g., sports psychology, change resulting from psychotherapy, and the entry of women into non-traditional math/science careers).

Bandura (1997) identified two related types of expectations that worked together to shape human behavior and influence performance outcomes. Self-efficacy expectations refer to individuals' beliefs about their abilities to execute specific behaviors and persist when confronted by obstacles that block their path. Related but separate from efficacy expectations, Bandura argued that outcome expectations also play a unique role in shaping human behavior. Outcome expectations highlight the beliefs we hold about the consequences that are likely to happen if certain behaviors are performed. For example, does a high school junior believe that if she gets good grades in her honors chemistry courses she will be able to major in chemistry in college and then find a rewarding career as a chemist in a company that would support her? Lent et al. described it this way. Self-efficacy expectations basically focus on the question "Can I do this?". Outcome expectations look at the perceived consequences of successfully doing these actions and ask the question "If I do this, what will happen?" (1994, p. 83).

A great deal of research in the career area has supported self-efficacy as one of the most important individual difference variables in the field. Counselors and parents are likely to hear the language of efficacy interwoven throughout the different strategies young people use to talk to others about their career goals, plans, ambitions, hopes, and fears. In particular, when working with young people, professionals are likely to hear four types of related efficacy expectation constructs (Lent et al., 1994). An example of what an adolescent might say about each of these four types is provided below.

1. Efficacy Expectations – "I am very confident that I can correctly solve this trigonometry problem."

2. Distal Outcome Expectations – "If I take extra math and science courses in high school, then I will be a lot better off when I start my two-year engineering technician community college program. That job pays great."

3. Process Outcome Expectations – "If I take these extra math courses, I am going to be in there by myself without my friends. But my parents will be pleased with me and help me."

4. Coping Self-Efficacy – "The tests the chemistry teacher gives are hard. I always run out of time and can't finish all the questions. I don't know what to do. I hate to admit it, but I don't think I can handle this."

In addition to efficacy expectations, career researchers

have found that the attributions we make play a key role in shaping the positive expectations young people need to achieve in the present, plan for postsecondary transitions, and pursue goals that lie far into the future. Weiner (1986) called attention to the inherent tendency human beings display to understand the world around us through interpreting the causes of these events. The interpretations that we make about the causes of our successes and failures then play a fundamental role in shaping our motivation and future actions. Weiner argued that every cause has three separate dimensions. The locus of the cause can be assigned to factors internal to ourselves (e.g., ability and talent) or to forces outside of ourselves (e.g., large scale economic trends like the oil embargo in the United States in the 1970s). We also look to see how stable the cause is and if it will change over time. Finally, we interpret events to see if the cause can be controlled by actions the person involved or others can take.

In summarizing the career research on the role of attributions, Luzzo and Jenkins-Smith (1998) concluded that there was clear evidence supporting the position that young people who use a more optimistic attributional style are more likely to be satisfied and successful in their careers. Advantages exist for individuals who interpret the causes of career-related events to be due to factors that are internal to the person, related to things that are controllable, and are likely to be unstable in that they can change over time. People who use more pessimistic attributional styles ascribe failure to themselves, think it will not change, and believe there is nothing they can do to make things better. This can lead to learned helplessness responses where individuals do not believe that they are able to bring about outcomes that they want. Career counseling professionals working with young people will hear the types of attributions students are making about their performance in present situations (e.g., in school and with friends) and how they are approaching future career goals. Examples of what an adolescent might say about the attributions they are using are provided below.

1. Locus Attributions – "I got a B+ on my last algebra test because I worked really hard and did all the practice homework problems."

2. Stability Attributions - "No way my parents can pay $25,000 for my college tuition. It doesn't matter how good my grades are."

3. Control Attributions – "I am not good at using computers. I just can't get better at this, so I might as well forget about using my art talent in making animations or doing advertising."

4. Optimistic Attributional Style – "Hey, you know what? I am smart enough to get good grades, pass this course, and graduate from my apprenticeship program. I have the ability; it is really up to me and that isn't going to change!"

Identity Development. Erikson (1968) emphasized that if a young person is going to be able to establish a stable ego identity in adulthood they will need to resolve their vocational identity issues in adolescence. He argued that through a collaborative process of exploration and goal formation a young person could come to make a commitment to pursue a career direction. This commitment would help to add purpose and direction to the young person's life and resolve for them the identity crisis of adolescence. Flum and Blustein (2000) argued that when a young person establishes a self-constructed career identity they accomplish the developmental challenge outlined by Erikson and position themselves to make a more successful transition into young adulthood.

Berzonsky (1992, 1993) described three identity statuses that adolescents establish in their attempt to resolve their identity crisis. First, he argued that some adolescents become diffused. They tend to approach the world in avoidant, fragmented, and poorly organized ways. Second, other adolescents have their identity conferred on them by custom, convention, and the dominating expectations of others. Individuals who create diffused and conferred identity statuses do not use a process of self-exploration to meet present demands and future opportunities. However, a third group uses active exploratory strategies to gather the information they need to make important life decisions. These information-oriented adolescents engage themselves in a self-directed process that results in the creation of an identity that is both flexible and autonomously chosen.

Building on the work of Berzonsky and Ryan and Deci (2000), Flum and Blustein (2000) argued that adolescents who adopt an active, exploratory strategy are more likely to create a self-constructed identity. In their words, these adolescents serve as the "authors" of their own becoming (p. 386). By internalizing such strategies for exploring careers and setting goals, these young people acquire a lifelong skill that they can use as they adapt to the changing network of roles and responsibilities that they will be called upon to successfully perform across their life spans. Flum and Blustein would suggest that at least one objective of any career guidance and counseling activity should be to help each young person to learn how to engage in exploratory activities that enable them to gather information they need about careers and training options. More importantly, career interventions should help each young person experience the awareness that they should be exploring the world to gather the information they need to make more self-directed choices about the kinds of possible futures they want to one day achieve.

Robbins and Kliewer (2000) summarized a vast body of research that has linked the creation and realization of self-defined goals with increased levels of subjective well being and satisfaction in adulthood. These goals provide the individual direction, organization, and purpose as they adapt to the present and move proactively towards future life contexts (Cantor & Sanderson, 1999). A review of the developmental literature suggests that career goals that enhance well being and life satisfaction in adulthood will have the following ten characteristics. These goals will be:

1. Firmly held, committed to, and consistently pursued.
2. Intrinsically valued by the person.
3. Autonomously chosen, as a result of the person being engaged in a serious process of exploration.
4. Clear and specific.
5. Both attainable and, at the same time, a challenge for the person to reach.
6. Closely connected to key decision points to help the person see what they need to do.
7. Connected to those specific behaviors that a person can bring under his/her voluntary control.
8. Realistic to one's daily life contexts, e.g., being a marine biologist in Missouri is not impossible, but it does present challenges if you want to live in the Midwestern part of the United States.
9. Can be nurtured and sustained by regular support from one's social contexts, e.g., home, school, and community.
10. Can be supported by available personal, social, and other tangible resources.

Person-Environment Fit. Working to help high school dropouts make more successful transitions into available occupations, Frank Parsons (1909) helped to launch the movement to provide vocational guidance and counseling services in the United States. His three-part model attempted to enhance the match or fit between the individual and their work environment. The first step was to assist individuals to better understand aspects of themselves that were important to their choice of a good occupation to enter (e.g., their abilities, interests, resources, and limitations). The second step was to help the young person learn about the critical features of different lines of work (e.g., job requirements, what it takes to be successful in different jobs, compensation, and available opportunities). After learning about themselves and the world of work, the counselor would help the individual through a process Parsons labeled "true reasoning." The effort of the counselor was to help clients enhance the match between their newly acquired self-knowledge and their now more detailed and accurate understanding of occupations. The hope was that, armed with more complete information about oneself and available employment opportunities, the young person would make a better decision about which job to enter. Better occupational choices would result in greater success and satisfaction in the world of work.

Parsons' work started what has come to be known as the "trait and factor" approach to career guidance and counseling services. As the dominant theoretical and practice paradigm in the field during the 20th century, trait and factor theorists continued to work out of Parsons' true reasoning framework. Individuals were understood to differ from each other in their possession and expression of traits such as personality orientation, work values, and talents and abilities. Careers were understood as differing around the patterns of traits that were required for success in those jobs. It was assumed that if a better match could be made between what is required in a job to be successful and the traits that an individual wants to and is capable of expressing in their work, the client would be able to make a better occupational decision. A more effective career decision would enhance the match between the person and the work environment. The prediction was made that more optimal matches would lead to better employment outcomes, such as job performance and job satisfaction.

During the 20th century, the trait and factor paradigm produced most of the leading theories in the field. Each model worked within Parsons' true reasoning and matching framework. Each theory articulated a different slant on what individuals should understand about themselves and the world of work. For example, John Holland (1997) argued that six personality types (i.e., Realistic, Investigative, Artistic, Social, Enterprising, and Conventional) play a pivotal role in career decision-making and occupational success. For Holland, occupational choices are an expression of the individual's underlying personality. People actively seek out employment possibilities that allow them to express personality traits that are important to them. In contrast, the Theory of Work Adjustment (Dawis & Lofquist, 1984) highlighted the connection between the preferred needs of employees and the reinforcements available in specific job environments. Work adjustment was then understood to be the dynamic and ongoing process by which workers try to maintain a level of correspondence that they find satisfying between what they need and what their work environment provides them. Greater levels of correspondence between worker needs and available environmental reinforcers would then lead to better work-related outcomes (e.g., better job performance, satisfaction, and fewer turnovers).

In the early part of his career, Donald Super (1970) introduced work values as a critical component for any comprehensive trait and factor theory. He contended that the assessment of an individual's work values (e.g., creativity, achievement, cultural identity, prestige, and autonomy) should be added to the emphasis on interests and abilities in trait and factor theories and assessments. It is important to note that research testing the predictive validity of leading trait and factor theories (the Theory of Work Adjustment and Holland's model) has so far been disappointing (e.g., Spokane, Meir, & Catalano, 2000). This is in part why we are arguing for a more comprehensive and integrative model of career development that allows for the inclusion of a much wider set of constructs that interact together to lead to better occupational outcomes.

Effective career guidance and counseling interventions help young people better understand themselves, explore the world of work, and go through a systematic decision-making process that integrates this growing awareness into an action plan. Young people benefit when they more clearly understand their: (a) personality orientations; (b) work values; (c) talents and abilities; (d) needs that are important to satisfy in their career; and (e) a wide range of career-related aspects that provide information necessary to making good career decisions (e.g., preferring to work indoors or outdoors; Gati, Fassa, & Mayer, 1998). In addition, young people need to really learn about the world of work. Accurate and up-to-date information is a vital component of effective interventions (Brown & Krane, 2000). Resources such as the ACT World of Work Map (2001) and free, online data sources (e.g., O*NET) make it practical and doable to provide current information to all students. And finally, decision-making models that help counselors assess the different kinds of decision-making difficulties that their students are struggling with (e.g., lack of readiness to make a decision because the person is not motivated, indecisive, or is burdened by debilitating beliefs) enable us to engage our students in exploratory discussions that realize the genuine intent of Parsons' process of "true reasoning."

Super et al. (1996) urged us to understand that choosing

a career is an act of creating meaning in our lives. In making such decisions, we are bringing to life a personally meaningful self-concept and making subjective decisions that eventually coalesce into purposeful life themes. This entails an ongoing effort where individuals attempt to optimize the fit between this subjective self and available occupational situations. By striving to enhance the match between self and career, we create the kind of future we hoped for and person we wanted to become.

Interests. Vocational interests have long been recognized as one of the cornerstones of career counseling (e.g., Kuder, 1939; Strong, 1927). For college students, interest scores have been found to predict between one-half to two-thirds of the variance in the actual occupations these young people enter (Harmon, Hansen, Borgen, & Hammer, 1994). Gifted adolescents entered college majors as predicted by interest tests that were taken ten years before these talented young people enrolled in college (Achter, Lubinski, Benbow, & Eftekhari-Sanjani, 1999). Workers living in different countries, but employed in the same occupations, are more alike in their interest patterns than adults who live in the same country, but work in different occupations (Fouad & Hansen, 1987). Interests express what we find intrinsically motivating (Ryan & Deci, 2000). In our experience as career counselors, researchers, and more importantly as parents, it is very clear that if you want to know what decisions a young person will make (e.g., courses to take, leisure activities, and colleges to attend) talk to them about their interests. The development of a proactive, resilient, and adaptive orientation is tied to young people finding their passion and deeply engaging themselves in the pursuit of activities they find to be intrinsically meaningful and rewarding.

Strong (1927, 1943) validated that one of the ways in which occupations differ from each other is in the pattern of interests exhibited by successful employees in those careers. The phrase "birds of a feather flock together and flocks are different from each other" has been used to call attention to the influence of interest patterns in job selection and success. More recently, researchers using data from twin studies have found that approximately one-third of the variance in measured interest scores can be explained genetically (Betsworth et al., 1994). However, it is important to note that the largest part of the variance in interest scores was explained by environmental experiences that are unique to the life events of the individual.

The environments that young people live in provide a "cafeteria of experience" that encourages or discourages the development of interests that originate from both genetic and environmental sources (Lykken et al., 1993). Talents can be nurtured and honed in one supportive environment, while prematurely limited and circumscribed in learning contexts that can be openly hostile or benignly neglectful. It is important to point out that while interest scores have been found to be quite stable over time, this stability has been statistically found at the group level (Swanson & Hansen, 1988). At the individual level, a person's pattern of interests can change dramatically. Career guidance and counseling services that provide a wide range of learning opportunities enable young people to express latent genetic interests as well as discover new preferences that add a vital and dynamic quality to their lives. Career guidance and counseling activities become an intentional strategy by which adults help young people to not prematurely circumscribe their aspirations and acquiesce to prevailing biases and stereotypes (e.g., gender, cultural, and racial biases; Gottfredson, 1981).

Self-Regulated Learning and Academic Achievement. Academic achievement is a primary conduit through which young people will establish valued places or marginalized economic lives in our technologically driven economy (Arbona, 2000). The consequences of not doing well in rigorous high school courses (like algebra and geometry) can be seen in the lowered college attendance rates of these students, especially students from low income families (e.g., U.S. Department of Education, 1997). The SCANS Report (U.S. Department of Labor and Secretary's Commission on Achieving Necessary Skills, 1991) outlined the skills young people needed to enter high-performance and high-pay workplaces. It is clear beyond any doubt that achieving academically and becoming a successful lifelong learner is a critical filter through which individual citizens and our country as a whole will secure our future economic well-being.

Assisting students to become self-regulated learners is one effective way that schools, families, and communities can help our young people achieve academically and become successful lifelong learners (Lapan, Kardash, & Turner, 2002). Self-regulated learning highlights the purposeful strategies that highly effective learners use to direct their thoughts, feelings, and actions to improve their performance in challenging learning contexts (Zimmerman & Schunk, 2001). Lapan et al. organized the research on self-regulated learning into a three-step process. Career guidance and counseling interventions can use this framework to improve the academic achievement of all students.

Step 1 rests on Zimmerman's (2000) insights into the intentional strategies effective learners use during the planning, performance, and outcome phases of important learning events. Self-regulated learners actively employ achievement-enhancing beliefs and performance enhancing self-instructional tactics. They regularly monitor their performance and alter their behavior as necessary. More successful learners routinely use effective learning strategies such as imagery, mnemonics, and the breaking down of tasks into their critical parts and then reconstructing the parts into a more meaningful whole. Finally, these learners set challenging and personally meaningful goals and standards for themselves.

Step 2 describes how more effective learners apply this active, purposeful approach to learning in activities that are both intrinsically and extrinsically motivating. Self-regulated learners internalize and integrate these strategies into the approach they take to any learning event, whether they like the subject matter or not. Unfortunately, students are not interested in a great deal of the subject matter they are required to learn. Ryan and Deci (2000) described a process by which externally motivated behavior (e.g., learning academic material that a student is not interested in) can be brought under self-determined control. More effective learners use the strategies outlined in Step 1 to internalize and integrate an approach to actively engage in the learning of material they find inherently interesting and more importantly to the subjects that they are much less interested in learning.

Step 3 is the direct outcome of the work more effective learners perform in Steps 1 and 2. These students are more fully engaged in their academic work. They have a greater self-investment and commitment to their studies. This greater engagement leads directly to better academic achievement (Marks, 2000). Success leads to greater personal satisfaction, well being, and the adoption of the skills and attitudes necessary to become a productive lifelong learner. For specific strategies on what schools, families, and communities can do to promote young people to become self-regulated learners, see Lapan (2004) and Lapan, Kardash, and Turner (2002).

Work Readiness Behaviors and Social Skills. The ability to get along and work productively with others is a cornerstone for future success and well being both in one's career and across the central life roles citizens perform in a pluralistic democracy. On the job, numerous studies have found that employees who build productive relationships with co-workers and supervisors experience greater job satisfaction, are less likely to leave that job, become more integrated into the organization, and have greater clarity about their role in the business (e.g., Wanberg & Kammeyer-Mueller, 2000). Lapan (2004) outlined how career guidance and counseling interventions should target at least six fundamental social skills and work readiness behaviors. These are: (a) social competence; (b) diversity skills; (c) positive work habits; (d) personal qualities; (e) personality and emotional states; and (f) entrepreneurship.

Social competence is a critical ingredient to emotional and physical well being in adulthood. The ability to build and maintain effective relationships is a critical on the job skill. Adults who can communicate well with others will have many more career opportunities and leadership roles open up to them. There is a growing awareness that caring for others and the environment are good for business and the world we live in (e.g., Richardson, 1998). On the job, the use of prosocial skills (i.e., helping, caring, and sharing behaviors that are intended to benefit others) enhances the value of these employees and assists the company to be more productive.

Cultural pluralism and the global marketplace require that workers embrace diversity and companies build culturally responsive workplaces (Lee, 2001). Young people need to become knowledgeable about differences between others. At the very least, they need to be able to be respectful and accepting of these differences. In the best of situations, the lives of individuals participating in effective learning communities and high performance work environments will be greatly enriched by these differences.

Young people who incorporate a range of positive work habits into their daily lives will be much more successful.

Developing a sense of personal industry assists young people to experience themselves as being useful and competent and leads to enhanced performance in young adulthood (Erikson, 1959; Vondracek, 1993). A sound work ethic keeps young people on course to finish the tasks they undertake in a high-quality manner. Demonstrating initiative is a key to success in any work context. Being responsible and using good judgment increases a worker's marketability and value to their organization.

There are a number of personal qualities that enhance success in the workplace. For example, individuals with more positive self-esteem and who in general hold a more favorable attitude about themselves will be more satisfied and productive. Having a positive attitude towards work and being open to new learning is an advantage. Personal hygiene (e.g., cleanliness and dress) and good self-presentation skills (e.g., making eye contact when appropriate) create positive relations with co-workers and supervisors.

Underlying personality and emotional states can circumscribe potential success. For example, the ability and willingness to speak in public is a valuable skill. However, fear of public speaking (our most common social phobia) leads many talented people to avoid these potentially career-enhancing situations (American Psychiatric Association, 1994). Difficulties with anxiety and depression can threaten our well being and productivity in all of the important life roles we perform. Behavioral and affective states like shyness have signficantly negative consequences for what individuals are able to do and achieve in their work lives (Phillips & Bruch, 1988).

And finally, the future growth of our economy is in the hands of entrepreneurs and small start up companies. Kourilsky and Walstad (2000) pointed to the growing interest young people are displaying to take more control over their lives by adopting a

43

"make your own job" attitude. By taking things in their own hands, young entrepreneurs are creating wealth that enriches all of us. For help in how to support young people to become entrepreneurs go to the Ewing Marion Kauffman Foundation website (www.emkf.org). Career guidance and counseling professionals develop interventions to assist young people to learn and use the wide range of social skills and work readiness behaviors that are required for success in high performing, high pay workplaces.

Summing Up

The integrative contextual model of career development makes it clear that strengths-based career guidance and counseling activities and services are central to the mission of every high performing school. They are not ancillary. Strengths-based career guidance and counseling activities and services, delivered through comprehensive guidance and counseling programs, focus on the fundamental developmental pathways leading young people to create personally valued futures that add meaning, purpose, direction, hope, and satisfaction to their lives. To empower young people to develop and use a proactive, resilient, and adaptive style, strengths-based career guidance and counseling activities and services help young people to develop six critical strengths: (a) have positive expectations; (b) explore, set goals, and create a self-defined identity; (c) better understand themselves, the world of work, and how to enhance the fit between themselves and future career options; (d) find and pursue their interests; (e) become a more successful student and self-regulated lifelong learner; and (f) get along better with others and develop a wide range of work readiness behaviors. These are the formative outcomes that career interventions should promote during the K-12 years. The development of these strength-based constructs lead directly to greater success in adulthood. The first step in developing and evaluating career guidance and counseling interventions is to clearly understand what the strength-based constructs are that we are trying to help all young people learn. The integrative contextual model of career development provides this foundation.

References

Achter, J. A., Lubinski, D., Benbow, C. P., & Eftekhari-Sanjani, H. (1999). Assessing vocational preferences among gifted adolescents adds incremental validity to abilities: A discriminant analysis of educational outcomes over a 10-year interval. *Journal of Educational Psychology, 91*(4), 777-786.

ACT. (1985). *Interim Psychometric Handbook for the Third Edition ACT Career Planning Program (Levels 1 and 2)*: The American College Testing Corporation.

American Psychiatric Association. (1994). *Diagnostic and statistical manual of mental disorders* (4th ed.). Washington, DC: Author.

Arbona, C. (2000). The development of academic achievement in school aged children: Precursors to career development. In S. D. Brown & R. W. Lent (Eds.), *Handbook of counseling psychology* (3rd ed., pp. 270-309). New York: Wiley.

Bandura, A. (1997). *Self-efficacy: The exercise of control*. New York: W.H. Freeman.

Berzonsky, M. D. (1992). A process perspective on identity and stress management. In G. R. Adams, T. P. Gullotta, & R. Montemayor (Eds.), *Adolescent identity formation* (Vol. 4, pp. 193-215). Newbury Park, CA: Sage.

Berzonsky, M. D. (1993). A constructivist view of identity development: People as postpositivist self-theorists. In J. Kroger (Ed.), *Discussions on ego identity* (pp. 169-203). Hillsdale, NJ: Erlbaum.

Betsworth, D. G., Bouchard, T. J., Cooper, C. R., Grotevant, H. D., Hansen, J. C., Scarr, S., et al. (1994). Genetic and environmental influences on vocational interests assessed using adoptive and biological families and twins reared apart and together. *Journal of Vocational Behavior, 44*(3), 263-278.

Bloch, D. P. (1996). Career development and workforce preparation: Educational policy versus school practice. *Career Development Quarterly, 45*(1), 20-40.

Blustein, D. L. (2006). *The Psychology of working: A new perspective for career development, counseling, and public policy.* Mahwah, NJ: Lawrence Erlbaum Associates, Inc.

Brown, S. D., & Krane, N. E. (2000). Four (or five) sessions and a cloud of dust: Old assumptions and new observations about career counseling. In S. D. Brown & R. W. Lent (Eds.), *Handbook of counseling psychology* (3rd ed., pp. 740-766). New York: John Wiley and Sons.

Cantor, N., & Sanderson, C. A. (1999). Life task participation and well-being: The importance of taking part in daily life. In D. Kahneman, E. Diener, & N. Schwarz (Eds.), *Well-being: The foundations of hedonic psychology* (pp. 230-243). New York: Russell-Sage.

Claes, R., & Ruiz-Quintanilla, S. (1998). Influences of early career experiences, occupational group, and national culture on proactive career behavior. *Journal of Vocational Behavior, 52*(3), 357-378.

Dawis, R. V., & Lofquist, L. H. (1984). *A psychological theory of work adjustment*. Minneapolis, MN: University of Minnesota Press.

Erikson, E. H. (1968). *Identity: youth and crisis*. New York: Norton.

Flum, H., & Blustein, D. L. (2000). Reinvigorating the study of vocational exploration: A framework for research. *Journal of Vocational Behavior, 56*(3), 380-404.

Fouad, N. A., & Hansen, J. C. (1987). Cross-cultural predictive accuracy of the Strong-Campbell Interest Inventory. *Measurement & Evaluation in Counseling & Development, 20*(1), 3-10.

Garner, R. (1990). When children and adults do not use learning strategies: Toward a theory of settings. *Review of Educational Research, 60*(4), 517-529.

Gati, I., Fassa, N., & Mayer, Y. (1998). An aspects-based approach to person-environment fit: A comparison between the aspect structure derived from characteristics of occupations and that derived from counselees' preferences. *Journal of Vocational Behavior, 53*, 28-43.

Gottfredson, L. S. (1981). Circumscription and compromise: A developmental theory of occupational aspirations. *Journal of Counseling Psychology, 28*(6), 545-579.

Gysbers, N. C., Heppner, M. J., & Johnston, J. A. (2009). *Career counseling: Process, issues, and techniques* (3rd ed.). Alexandria, VA: American Counseling Association.

Harmon, L. W., Hansen, J. I., Borgen, F. H., & Hammer, A. L. (1994). *Strong Interest Inventory: Applications and technical guide* (5th ed.). Palo Alto, CA: Consulting Psychologists Press.

Holland, J. L. (1997). *Making vocational choices: A theory of
vocational personalities and work environments* (3rd ed.).
Odessa, FL: Psychological Assessment Resources.

Kourilsky, M. L., & Walstad, W. B. (2000). *The E generation.
Prepared for the entrepreneurial economy?* Dubuque, IA:
Kendall/Hunt Publishing Company.

Kuder, F. (1939). *Kuder Preference Record-Personal, Form A.*
Chicago: University of Chicago Bookstore.

Lapan, R. T. (2004). *Career development across the K-16 years:
Connecting the present to satisfying and successful futures.*
Alexandria, VA: American Counseling Association.

Lapan, R. T., Aoyagi, M., & Kayson, M. (2007). Helping rural
adolescents make successful post-secondary transitions: A
3-year longitudinal study. *Professional School Counseling,
10*(3), 266-272.

Lapan, R. T., Kardash, C. M., & Turner, S. (2002). Empowering
students to become self-regulated learners. *Professional
School Counseling, 5*, 257-265.

Lapan, R. T., Osana, H. P., Tucker, B., & Kosciulek, J. F. (2002).
Challenges for creating community career partnerships:
Perspectives from practitioners. *The Career Development
Quarterly, 51*, 172-190.

Lee, C. C. (2001). Culturally responsive school counselors and
programs: Addressing the needs of all students.
Professional School Counseling, 4(4), 257-261.

Lent, R. W., Brown, S. D., & Hackett, G. (1994). Toward a
unifying social cognitive theory of career and academic
interest, choice, and performance. *Journal of Vocational
Behavior, 45*(1), 79-122.

Lent, R. W., Brown, S. D., & Hackett, G. (2000). Contextual
supports and barriers to career choice: A social cognitive
analysis. *Journal of Counseling Psychology, 47*(1), 36-49.

Luzzo, D. A., & Jenkins-Smith, A. (1998). Development and initial validation of the Assessment of Attributions for Career Decision-Making. *Journal of Vocational Behavior, 52*(2), 224-245.

Lykken, D. T., Bouchard, T., McGue, M., & Tellegen, A. (1993). Heritability of interests: A twin study. *Journal of Applied Psychology, 78*(4), 649-661.

Marks, H. M. (2000). Student engagement in instructional activity: Patterns in the elementary, middle, and high school years. *American Educational Research Journal, 37*(1), 153-184.

Markus, H., & Nurius, P. (1986). Possible selves. *American Psychologist, 41*(9), 954-969.

Mitchell, K. E., Levin, A. S., & Krumboltz, J. D. (1999). Planned happenstance: Constructing unexpected career opportunities. *Journal of Counseling and Development, 77*(2), 115-124.

Parsons, F. (1909). *Choosing a vocation.* Boston: Houghton-Mifflin.

Phillips, S. D., & Bruch, M. A. (1988). Shyness and dysfunction in career development. *Journal of Counseling Psychology, 35*(2), 159-165.

Richardson, M. S. (1998). Counseling in uncertainty: Empowerment through work and relation practices. *Educational and Vocational Guidance, 62,* 2-8.

Robbins, S. B., & Kliewer, W. L. (2000). Advances in theory and research on subjective well-being. In S. D. Brown & R. Lent (Eds.), *Handbook of counseling psychology* (3rd ed., pp. 310-345). New York: Wiley.

Ryan, R. M., & Deci, E. L. (2000). Self-determination theory and the facilitation of intrinsic motivation, social development, and well-being. *American Psychologist, 55*(1), 68-78.

Savickas, M. L. (1997). Career adaptability: An integrative construct for life-span, life-space theory. *Career Development Quarterly, 45*(3), 247-259.

Schlossberg, N. K., Waters, E. B., & Goodman, J. (1995). *Counseling adults in transition: Linking practice with theory* (2nd ed.). New York: Springer.

School-To-Work Opportunities Act, Pub. L. No. 103-289 (1994).

Spokane, A. R. (1985). A review of research on person-environment congruence in Holland's theory of careers. *Journal of Vocational Behavior, 26*(3), 306-343.

Spokane, A. R., Meir, E. I., & Catalano, M. (2000). Person-environment congruence and Holland's theory: A review and reconsideration. *Journal of Vocational Behavior, 57*(2), 137-187.

Strong, E. K., Jr. (1927). *Vocational Interest Blank.* Palo Alto, CA: Stanford University Press.

Strong, E. K., Jr. (1943). *Vocational interests of men and women.* Stanford, CA: Stanford University Press.

Super, D. E. (1954). Career patterns as a basis for vocational counseling. *Journal of Counseling Psychology, 1*, 12-20.

Super, D. E. (1970). *Work values inventory manual.* Chicago: Riverside Publishing Company.

Super, D. E., Savickas, M. L., & Super, C. M. (1996). The life-span, life-space approach to careers. In D. Brown, L. Brooks & Associates (Eds.), *Career choice and development* (3rd ed., pp. 121-178). San Francisco: Jossey-Bass.

Swanson, J. L., & Fouad, N. A. (1999). Applying theories of person-environment fit to the transition from school to work. *Career Development Quarterly, 47*(4), 337-347.

Tranberg, M., Slane, S., & Ekeberg, S. E. (1993). The relation between interest congruence and satisfaction: A metaanalysis. *Journal of Vocational Behavior, 42*(3), 253-264.

U.S. Department of Education. (1997). *Mathematics equals opportunity.* White Paper prepared for the U. S. Secretary of Education Richard W. Riley. Washington, DC: Author.

U. S. Department of Labor & Secretary's Commission on Achieving Necessary Skills. (1991). *What work requires of schools: A SCANS report for America 2000.* Washington, DC: Author.

Vondracek, F. W. (1993). Vocational identity development in adolescence. In R. K. Silbereisen & E. Todt (Eds.), *Adolescence in context: The interplay of family, school, peers, and work in adjustment* (pp. 284-303). New York: Springer.

Wanberg, C. R., & Kammeyer-Mueller, J. D. (2000). Predictors and outcomes of proactivity in the socialization process. *Journal of Applied Psychology, 85*, 373–385.

Weiner, B. (1986). *An attributional theory of motivation and emotion.* New York: Springer-Verlag.

Zimmerman, B. J. (2000). Attaining self-regulation: A social cognitive perspective. In M. Boekaerts, P. R. Pintrich, & M. Zeidner (Eds.), *Handbook of self-regulation* (pp. 13-39). New York: Academic Press.

Zimmerman, B. J., & Schunk, D. H. (Eds.) (2001). *Self-regulated learning and academic achievement: Theoretical perspectives* (2nd ed.). Mahwah, NJ: Lawrence Erlbaum Associates.

Part II.
An Organizational Framework
and Evidence-Based Activities

Chapter 3

Comprehensive Guidance and Counseling Programs: A Framework for Delivering Strengths-Based Career Development

Careers education must enable students in their imagination of possible selves in possible futures. And it must do that for a long-life life-long pursuit. But it can't be a collection of things to learn, it is – rather – for enabling students to take their own command of learning processes. It is therefore expressed not in pre-scripted nouns but in learning verbs. (Law, 2007, p. 1)

There are three parts to this chapter. Part One reviews the historical origins of, as well as the overall structure for, comprehensive guidance and counseling programs. The relationship between the guidance curriculum component of comprehensive programs and career development content is described. Part Two presents strengths-based career development content developed from the integrative contextual model of career development. Part Three outlines how strengths-based career development content is delivered through the four program components of comprehensive programs (Guidance Curriculum, Individual Planning, Responsive Services, and Systems Support).

A holistic view is provided that unites and fully integrates personal/social development and academic development with strengths-based career development content that is optimally delivered through comprehensive guidance and counseling programs.

Part One:
Comprehensive Guidance and Counseling Programs

Guidance and counseling in the schools has changed rapidly in the last three decades, from a position-services model to a comprehensive program firmly grounded in principles of human growth and development. Guidance and counseling in the schools has become a developmental program focusing on prevention as well as remediation. As a developmental program it has a content base consisting of knowledge, skills, and attitudes that contribute to overall student development and success. It also has an organizational framework, resources, and processes to fully implement the program. As a developmental program, guidance and counseling is an integral part of education and is, as a result, an equal partner with other instructional programs in education.

Traditionally, however, guidance and counseling was not conceptualized and implemented in this manner because, as Aubrey (1973) suggested, guidance and counseling was seen as a support service lacking a content base and an organizational framework of its own. Sprinthall (1971) made this same point when he stated that there was little content in the practice of guidance and counseling and that guidance and counseling textbooks usually avoided discussion of a subject matter base and an organizational framework for guidance and counseling programs.

If guidance and counseling is to become an equal partner

in education with other instructional programs and if guidance and counseling is able to meet the increasingly complex needs of individuals and society, it is our opinion that it must become a program conceptually and organizationally with its own content base and organizational structure. The call for this is not new; many early pioneers in the past century issued the same call. But the call was not loud enough during the early years, and, as a result, guidance and counseling was first organized as a position and then a service with an emphasis on duties, processes, and techniques. The need and the call for guidance and counseling to become a program continued to emerge occasionally thereafter, but not until the late 1960s and early 1970s did it reemerge and become visible in the form of a developmental comprehensive program (Gysbers & Henderson, 2006).

Program Framework

Today, in the United States, the major way to organize guidance activities and services in schools is the comprehensive guidance and counseling program (American School Counselor Association, 2005; Gysbers & Henderson, 2006; Johnson & Johnson, 2001; Myrick, 2003). The use of the comprehensive guidance and counseling program approach began in the 1980s (Gysbers & Moore, 1981), based on work undertaken in the 1970s (Gysbers & Moore, 1974), as well as the work of Johnson and Johnson (2001) and Myrick (2003). In 2003 the American School Counselor Association (ASCA) endorsed the concept by publishing the ASCA National Model (ASCA, 2005).

A comprehensive guidance and counseling program, as described by Gysbers and Henderson (2006), consists of four elements: content, organizational framework, resources, and development, management, and accountability. The content element identifies the knowledge, skills, and attitudes considered important by school districts for students to master as a result of their participation in the district's comprehensive guidance and counseling program. The organizational framework contains three structural components (definition, rationale, assumptions), four program components (guidance curriculum, individual student planning, responsive services, system support), along with a suggested distribution of school counselor time by grade levels across the four program components. The resource element consists of the human, financial, and political resources required to fully implement the program. The last element, development, management, and accountability describes the phases of putting a comprehensive program into full operation as well as evaluating and enhancing the program once it has been implemented (See Figure 3-1 for a diagram of the framework).

Program Content

In all comprehensive guidance and counseling programs today, knowledge, skills, and attitudes focusing on career development are part of the content elements of these programs. Most often such content is grouped under a domain called career. Additional knowledge, skills, and attitudes that are vital to career guidance and counseling are usually grouped under the domains of academic and personal/social.

The idea of career development content (knowledge, skills, attitudes) is not new. Consider, for example, Parsons' (1909) formulation of vocational guidance.

Comprehensive Guidance and Counseling Programs: A Framework
for Delivering Strengths-Based Career Development

Figure 3-1

Comprehensive Guidance and Counseling Program Elements

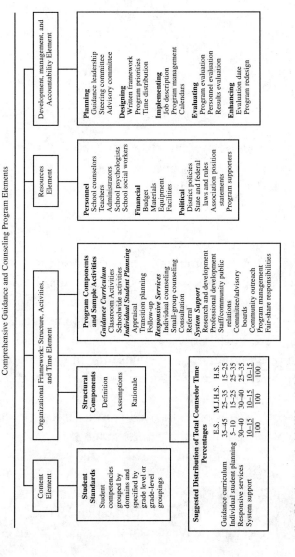

Note. E.S. = elementary school; M.J.H.S. = middle/junior high school; H.S. = high school.

Note: From *Developing & managing your school guidance and counseling program*, by N. C. Gysbers and P. Henderson, 2006, Alexandria, VA: American Counseling Association. Copyright 2006 by the American Counseling Association. Reprinted with permission.

> In the wise choice of a vocation there are three broad factors: (1) a clear understanding of yourself, your aptitudes, abilities, interests, ambitions, resources, limitations, and their causes; (2) a knowledge of the requirements and conditions of success, advantages and disadvantages, compensation, opportunities, and prospects in different lines of work; (3) true reasoning on the relations of these two groups of facts. (p. 5)

Notice that Parsons stated that students needed self understanding, they needed knowledge about the work world, and they needed to be skilled in decision making or true reasoning as he called it.

Then later, Davis (1914) inaugurated a plan to teach vocational guidance through the English curriculum covering such topics as vocational ambition, the value of education, the elements of character that make for success, the world's work—a call to service, choosing a vocation, and preparation for one's life work. As the decades unfolded, topics such as these were taught through various curricula and/or through stand alone courses. As a result, guidance and counseling in the schools has had a content base focusing on career development and career guidance and counseling from the very beginning.

Work on establishing today's content base for career guidance and placement began in earnest in the 1960s as a part of national and state efforts to evaluate guidance and counseling work in the schools (O'Hare, 1969-70; Wellman & Moore, 1975). It was also undertaken due to a renewed interest in vocational guidance (career guidance) and its theoretical foundation, career development.

In 1971, the state of Wisconsin published *A K-12 Guide for Integrating Career Development into Local Curriculum*

(Wisconsin Department of Public Instruction, 1971). This guide organized student outcomes into three domains, namely self, work world, and career planning and preparation with a focus on a broad outcome of emerging self and vocational identity. In the same year the California State Department of Education published *Career Guidance: A California Model for Career Development K-Adult* (1971). The focus of career guidance in this model was students' emerging career identity with three domains of student outcomes. The outcomes were career planning and decision making, life styles and personal satisfaction, and education, work and leisure alternatives. Later, in 1974 Gysbers and Moore published *Career Guidance, Counseling and Placement: Elements of an Illustrative Program Guide*. In it they identified a model that had four domains as organizers for student outcomes. Their domains included self knowledge and interpersonal skills; life roles, settings, and events; life career planning knowledge and skills; and basic studies and occupational preparation.

From the 1970s onward, states across the country began developing state models/guides to develop and implement comprehensive guidance programs. Included in these models and guides were taxonomies of student outcomes grouped into domains. A domain emphasizing career development and career guidance and counseling was always present.

In addition to work on identifying and categorizing the content base for career guidance and counseling at the state and local levels, national organizations also have been involved in this process. For example, America's Career Resource Network published *The National Career Development Guidelines* (2006). The American School Counselor Association (ASCA) also published a list of student outcomes with one domain being career development (Campbell & Dahir, 1997).

The National Career Development Guidelines used the titles Personal Social Development, Educational Achievement and Lifelong Learning, and Career Management to organize learning outcomes. Goals were then identified for each group of learning outcomes. Learning stages including Knowledge Acquisition, Application, and Reflection were used to identify the phases of learning. Finally, indicators of specific learning outcomes were provided coded by domain, learning stage, and then numerically.

In 2005 ASCA published the second edition of *The ASCA National Model: A Framework for School Counseling.* In it the content domains of academic, career, and person/social development drawn from the work of Campbell and Dahir (1997) were presented. ASCA used the term standards to identify broad areas of learning followed by specific learnings titled competencies and indicators. The grade groupings of K-2, 3-5, 6-8, and 9-12 are used to display the learning sequence of the standards, competencies, and indicators.

National and State Standards for Program Content

Today the ASCA National Model (2005), all state models, and all local school district models for comprehensive guidance and counseling programs as well as the National Career Development Guidelines (2006) feature career guidance and counseling content for students to master grouped under the domain of career or a related title. These models also feature content related to career grouped under the domains of academic and personal/social. Corresponding to other educational disciplines the content in these domains is increasingly being cast as standards. The standards are then subdivided into smaller units and are displayed by grade level or by grade level groupings as goals, indicators, or grade level expectations.

The use of the word standards to describe the knowledge,

skills, and attitudes students acquire from their participation in comprehensive guidance and counseling programs is designed to align these programs with other instructional programs in education. What are guidance standards? ASCA (2005) defined them as 'those statements providing a description of what students should know and be able to do at the highest level of expectation" (p. 32). Thus, the content base for guidance and counseling consists of a number of standards each indicating a particular aspect of knowledge and skill students should acquire organized into the three domains of career development, academic development, and personal/social development.

How many guidance content standards are required in each domain? Enough standards are required to insure that the body of knowledge and skills embodied in each domain is covered adequately. A review of national and state models reveals that the number of standards varies depending upon how those aspects of human growth and development to which guidance and counseling contributes are interpreted.

While the ASCA National Model (2005) and many states use the three domains of career, academic, and personal/social to group standards, some states and national organizations use more than three domains while others use three domains, but with different titles. Examples of national and state standards are presented below.

ASCA National Standards
Academic Development
A. Students will acquire the attitudes, knowledge and skills contributing to effective learning in school and across the lifespan.
B. Students will complete school with the academic preparation essential to choose from a wide range of substantial post-secondary options, including college.

C. Students will understand the relationship of academics to the world of work and to life at home and in the community.

Career Development
A. Students will acquire the skills to investigate the world of work in relation to knowledge of self and to make informed career decisions.
B. Students will employ strategies to achieve future career goals with success and satisfaction.
C. Students will understand the relationship between training and the world of work.

Personal/Social Development
A. Students will acquire the knowledge, attitude and interpersonal skills to help them understand and respect self and others.
B. Students will make decisions, set goals and take necessary action to achieve goals.
C. Students will understand safety and survival skills. (American School Counselor Association, 2005)

The Missouri Comprehensive Guidance Program Content Standards

Personal and Social Development

In the Comprehensive Guidance Program, students in Missouri Public Schools will acquire personal and social knowledge needed for:

CG1 understanding self as an individual and as a member of diverse local and global communities.

CG2 interacting with others in ways that respect individual and group differences.

CG3 applying personal safety skills and coping skills.

Academic Development

In the Comprehensive Guidance Program, students in Missouri Public Schools will acquire the knowledge of academic development needed for:

> CG4 applying the skills for educational achievement.
>
> CG5 applying the skills of transitioning between educational levels.
>
> CG6 developing and monitoring personal educational plans.

Career Development

In the Comprehensive Guidance Program, students in Missouri Public Schools will acquire career development knowledge needed for:

> CG7 applying career exploration and planning skills in the achievement of life career goals.
>
> CG8 knowing where and how to obtain information about the world of work and post-secondary training/education.
>
> CG9 applying employment readiness skills and the skills for on-the-job success.
>
> (Gysbers, Stanley, Kosteck-Bunch, Magnuson, & Starr, 2008, pp. 80-83)

Part Two:
Strengths-Based Career Development Content

A Holistic Approach

    The integrative contextual model of career development presented in Chapter 2 is a holistic theory that unites the academic, career, and personal-social content domains of comprehensive guidance and counseling programs. By helping all K-12 students to develop and use strengths-based career development strategies to interact in school, home, and their community, professional school counselors can unite the three content domains of comprehensive programs and ensure students will master standards essential for life long success. Academic development and personal/social development are not distinct and separate from career development. These content domains are not three isolated silos. They are intimately intertwined developmental processes that work together to assist young people to develop proactive, resilient, and adaptive approaches to the present and personally-valued futures.

> To be successful in school and in life, students need not only to master academic content, but also to learn to understand and manage their emotions, be responsible and caring, exercise good judgment and make sound decisions, be able to make healthy choices and resolve conflicts, and be prepared to contribute to their community as constructive, committed and effective citizens. (Zins, Elias, & Greenberg, 2007, p. 79)

Professional school counselors who use strengths-based career development content to develop career guidance and counseling activities help students master all nine content standards recommended by ASCA across the domains of academic development, career development, and personal/social development. Strengths-based career development content integrates these three content domains to help students learn the knowledge, attitudes, and skills essential for success across the changing opportunities and challenges of their life spans. It provides the specific learning tasks students need to master if they are to meet national and state standards. For example, the

ASCA National Model content standards (2005) provide general, overarching goals for what students should learn through their participation in their schools' comprehensive program. Standard A under Career Development directs professional school counselors to help all students "acquire the skills to investigate the world of work in relation to knowledge of self and to make informed career decisions" (p. 104). What is not stated are the specific investigative skills needed, what parts of self students should become aware of, and a goal setting strategy linked to an information seeking process of identity development that is necessary if adolescents are to be empowered to make informed career decisions.

The strengths-based career development content that is described below provides the fundamental building blocks essential for mastering each ASCA content standard in the academic, career, and personal-social domains. It unites the standards in these three content domains in the holistic, intentional, and organized work of professional school counselors. The career development content details what all students should know and be able to do if they are to master each standard of the three domains at the highest level of expectation, as recommended by ASCA.

The strengths-based career development content has a specific academic focus like all other instructional programs in education. For example, if a student does not know what a quadratic equation is and how it can be used as a tool to solve problems, then we can conclude that there are significant gaps in their knowledge of algebra. In the same way, if a student uses lowered self-efficacy expectations and a pessimistic attributional style to plan their postsecondary education, then we can conclude that there is a significant gap in their knowledge and ability to "employ strategies to achieve future career goals with success and satisfaction" (ASCA National Standard B under Career Development, 2005, p. 104). The use of embedded strengths-based career development content moves a comprehensive program from an ancillary support service to an instructional program central to the success of each student in every effective school.

Table 3-1

Strengths-Based Career Development Content from the Integrative Contextual Model of Career Development

Overall Goal: **Helping All Students to Become Proactive, Resilient, and Adaptive Adults**

Positive Orientation

1. **Direction:** Students can describe in detail a postsecondary educational and career direction that they are very interested in and highly motivated to pursue

2. **Commitment:** Students are committed to pursuing specific postsecondary educational and career paths

3. **Preparation:** Students are effectively preparing themselves to successfully achieve their postsecondary educational and career goals

4. **Initiative:** Students show initiative and take advantage of opportunities that will help them to successfully reach their educational and career goals

5. **Assertiveness:** Students take charge and assertively do what needs to be done in order to successfully reach their educational and career goals

6. **Hopefulness:** Students are very hopeful that they will one day work in a career where they will be happy and satisfied

Objective 1: **Positive Expectations**

Components: Self-efficacy beliefs, Distal outcome beliefs, Process outcome beliefs, Coping self-efficacy beliefs, and Optimistic attribution style

Strengths

1. **Self-efficacy for challenging barriers:** Students are confident in their ability to successfully deal with challenges they perceive they may have to face when attempting to reach their educational and career goals

2. **Self-efficacy for educational requirements and job duties:** Students are confident that they could successfully master both the educational requirements and job duties necessary to work in careers that they are interested in pursuing

3. **Outcome expectations:** Students are confident that if they successfully prepare themselves to enter a career they are interested in, then there is nothing that will get in their way from entering a satisfying job in that career (e.g., prejudice related to sex-role biases or ethnic/racial discrimination)

4. **Locus attributions:** Students believe that what will really help them to be successful in reaching their educational and career goals comes mostly from inside of themselves (like their talents and effort)

5. **Stability attributions:** Students believe that they can solve the problems that might get in their way as they try to reach their educational and career goals

6. **Control attributions:** Students believe that they can control potential problems that might get in their way as they try to reach their educational and career goals

Objective 2: **Identity Development**

Components: Exploration and information seeking, Goal development, and Commitment to an autonomously chosen, self-defined educational and career direction

Strengths

1. **Specific and clearly defined goals:** Students' educational and career goals are both clearly defined and specific

2. **Difficult and challenging goals:** Students have set educational and career goals that are both difficult and challenging

3. **Goals that identify actions to be taken:** Students' goals help them to see what they need to do in order to reach their career dreams

4. **Career exploration:** Students have participated in extensive career exploration activities that have helped them to seriously reflect on their educational and career choices and the postsecondary directions they might want to pursue

5. **Meaningful and valued career direction:** Students have made significant progress in identifying a career direction and postsecondary educational opportunities that they see as being personally meaningful and valuable to them

6. **Self-defined choices:** Students can discuss in some depth the career options that they are defining and committing themselves to pursue

Objective 3: **Understanding Yourself and the World of Work**

Components: Personality orientations, work values, interests, talents and abilities, needs important to satisfy in a career, and career-related aspects necessary for making a good career decision

Strengths

1. **Personality Orientations:** Students know what aspects of their personality that they want to express in a future career and the kinds of careers that would encourage them to use these personal characteristics

2. **Work Values:** Students know what work values are important to them and the kinds of careers that would encourage them to express these values

3. **Abilities, Talents, and Skills:** Students know what abilities, talents, and skills they want to use in a future career and the kinds of careers that would require them to use these abilities, talents, and skills

4. **Interests:** Students know what career interests they are passionate about pursuing and the kinds of careers that would encourage them to develop these interests

5. **Working conditions:** Students know what kinds of working conditions they prefer in a career and the kinds of careers that would provide this to them

6. **Match between self-understanding and the world of work:** Students have found an educational and career direction that has real potential to create an optimal match between who they are as a person and those work environments that would support and encourage them to be that kind of person

Objective 4: **Becoming a Successful Student and a Self-Regulated Lifelong Learner**

Components: Self-regulated learning skills, Learning strategies, and Academic performance

Strengths

1. **Needed academic skills:** Students have developed the needed academic skills to be successful in their pursuit of postsecondary educational and career goals

2. **Language Arts classes:** Students have mastered their language arts classes

3. **Mathematics classes:** Students have mastered their mathematics classes

4. **Science and Technology classes:** Students have mastered their science and technology classes

5. **Interesting academic direction:** Students have found an intrinsically interesting academic direction to pursue

6. **Self-regulated learner:** Students have become effective self-regulated learners who are actively engaged and committed to succeed in their K-12 schools and postsecondary educational settings

<u>Objective 5:</u> **Getting Along with Others and Developing Work Readiness Behaviors**

<u>Components:</u> Social competence, Diversity skills and attitudes, Positive work habits, Personal qualities, Emotional states, and Entrepreneurship

<u>Strengths</u>

1. **Communication and social skills:** Students can effectively communicate, be empathic towards, and get along with others

2. **Diversity skills and attitudes:** Students are knowledgeable of, respectful of, accepting of, and enriched by the differences (e.g., cultural, ethnic, racial, sexual, and global) between people in their community, throughout their country, and across the globe

3. **Responsible work habits:** Students use responsible work habits (e.g., showing initiative, following rules and regulations, being dependable, and completing tasks on one's own and under the supervision of others) to be successful in school, at home, and in their community

4. **Positive personal qualities:** Students use positive personal qualities (e.g., being a leader, having positive self-esteem, and presenting themselves in a positive manner) to be successful in school, at home, and in their community

5. **Emotional balance:** Students approach school, home, friends, and their community with emotional balance (e.g., they are not overly troubled by feelings of fear, sadness, shyness, or anger)

6. **Entrepreneurship:** Students know how to start, own, and operate their own businesses

Objective 6: **Find and Follow Your Interests and Your Passions**

Components: Exploring the four domains of the ACT World of Work Map (DATA, IDEAS, PEOPLE, and THINGS)

Strengths

1. **DATA work tasks:** Students have extensively explored careers that would require them to work with facts, records, files, and numbers (e.g., purchasing agents, accountants, and air traffic controllers)

2. **IDEAS work tasks:** Students have extensively explored careers that would require them to work with theories, abstractions, knowledge, insights, and find new ways to express things (e.g., scientists, musicians, and writers)

3. **PEOPLE work tasks:** Students have extensively explored careers that would require them to help others. These careers might include informing, serving, persuading, entertaining,

directing, and motivating others (e.g., teachers, salespersons, and nurses)

4. **THINGS work tasks:** Students have extensively explored careers that would require them to work with machines, mechanisms, materials, and tools, as well as physical and biological processes (e.g., electricians, technicians, and engineers).

Part Three: The Delivery System

How is strengths-based career development content provided to all students K-12? It is provided to all students K-12 through the comprehensive guidance and counseling programs' components of guidance curriculum, individual student planning, responsive services, and systems support. Classroom guidance curriculum provides K-12 activities to all students to assist them to achieve strengths-based career development content objectives. Individual student planning focuses on helping all students use the strengths- based content they have learned in the guidance curriculum to develop and use life career plans or personal plans of study to progress towards personally-valued postsecondary educational and career goals. Responsive services are available to students whose personal circumstances, concerns, or problems are threatening to interfere with or are interfering with their ability to achieve strengths-based career development content outcomes. And finally, systems support activities enable professional school counselors to build bridges that connect students to the dynamic world of work learning experiences through such vehicles as community career partnerships.

Guidance Curriculum

Before a description of the guidance curriculum of a comprehensive program is presented, it is first necessary to define what a curriculum is and what a curriculum is based upon. Wiggins and McTighe (1998) defined a curriculum as "a specific blueprint for learning that is derived from content and performance standards" (p. 4). Squires (2005), on the other hand, defined curriculum as a document that "describes (in writing) the most important outcomes of the schooling process; thus, the curriculum is a document in which resides the district's 'collected wisdom' about what is most important to teach" (p. 3). It is also important to remember that a curriculum is discipline specific; hence, we have a guidance curriculum as part of a comprehensive guidance and counseling program.

What is the basis for a curriculum? According to Squires (2005), a "curriculum is based on standards" (p. 3). Standards usually describe appropriate content to be mastered by students over a range of grade levels. For guidance and counseling, as you have seen, standards are typically grouped under domain titles such as career, academic, and personal/social and identify the attitudes, beliefs, knowledge, and skills important for students to acquire as they progress through grades K-12. By implementing a guidance curriculum, infused with strengths-based career development content, professional school counselors are assisting all students to master local, state, or national content standards.

The idea of a guidance curriculum is not new, particularly one that focuses on career guidance and counseling. As previously noted, Davis (1914) had outlined such a curriculum in the early 1900s. Of more immediate interest, however, is the work of Tennyson, Soldahl, and Mueller (1965) entitled *The Teacher's Role in Career Development* and the Airlie House Conference in May 1966 on the topic "Implementing Career Development Theory and Research Through the Curriculum," which was sponsored by the National Vocational Guidance Association (Ashcroft, 1966). Later in the 1960s and early 1970s came the work of such theorists and practitioners as Gysbers (1969), Herr (1969), and Hansen (1970), all of whom spoke to the need to integrate career development concepts into the curriculum. Through these efforts and others like them, career development concepts began to be translated into individual outcomes and the resulting goals and objectives arranged sequentially, K-12.

Today, all state comprehensive school guidance and

counseling program models and all local school district programs contain a guidance curriculum component with career development as a major domain. Career guidance and counseling activities begin in elementary school with classroom units emphasizing career awareness. At the middle and high school levels a wide variety of career awareness, exploration, planning, and transition activities take place. Classroom presentations, career/educational days and nights, job shadowing, and the exploration of accurate and up to date career information are just a few examples of the types of career guidance and counseling activities that are now widely available in many schools (Parsad, Alexander, Farris, & Hudson, 2003).

Individual Student Planning

Individual student planning is not a new idea either. A major goal of career guidance and counseling over the years has been to assist students to think about and plan for their futures. However, no specific structure was provided that mandated individual student planning. That changed when Gysbers and Moore (1981) introduced the idea that individual student planning should be a major component of comprehensive guidance and counseling programs along with guidance curriculum, responsive services, and system support. To facilitate the application of this component to practice, Gysbers (1985) developed a training module "Create and Use an Individual Career Development Plan" to train professional school counselors on how to assist students in their career planning.

In the 1990s the importance of individual student planning was demonstrated by a study of young people in Indiana titled *High Hopes Long Odds: Next Steps*. The study found that:

The difference in the high school experiences of students with plans for 4 years of high school courses and career plans versus students without such counselor-assisted plans was so great that providing help with these plans must be offered at every school. (Orfield & Paul, 1994, p. 11)

Is individual student planning still important today? Will it be important in the future? Pellitteri, Stern, Shelton, and Muller-Ackerman (2006) answered these questions by stating that:

Many students are unaware of how critical this skill, goal setting and planning, is to a full, rewarding, and successful life . . . . goals give us our bearing and point us in a purposeful direction. (pp. 209-210)

To illustrate the importance of individual student planning, several states have passed legislation requiring or recommending that individual student planning activities take place in schools. For example, in 1996 and 1997, the state of Utah (Utah State Statute for Comprehensive Guidance, 1996; Utah State Board of Education Administrative Rules for Comprehensive Guidance, 1997) translated the idea of individual plans for students into state law and state board of education policy requiring that all students develop and implement personalized student education/occupation plans.

The state of Washington passed a law similar to the rule passed by the state of Utah that encourages schools to help students develop and use plans of study (Washington State House Bill 2423, 2006). In addition, the state of Missouri required that an individual student planning system be in place in school no later than eighth grade and that it include the necessary planning forms and procedures (Missouri School Improvement Program, 2003).

At about the same time that Utah passed legislation to require individual student planning, the National Association of Secondary School Principals (1996) published a report titled *Breaking Ranks*. In it they recommended that each student in high school develop and use a personal plan for progress. The importance of individual student planning was emphasized again with the publication of *Breaking Ranks II* (National Association of Secondary School Principals, 2004). Recommendation 12 stated:

> Each student will have a Personal Plan for Progress that will be reviewed often to ensure that the high school takes individual needs into consideration and to allow students, within reasonable parameters, to design their own methods for learning in an effort to meet high standards. (p. 84)

The idea behind personalized learning is that it "allows the student to understand who he or she is, what adult roles seem most desirable, and how to get from here to there in the most productive way" (p. 169).

In *Breaking Ranks in the Middle* (National Association of Secondary School Principals, 2006), individual student planning was also stressed. The report recommended that sixth or seventh graders and their parents be introduced to planning for their education and beyond. The report also emphasized the need for students to meet frequently and meaningfully with an adult to plan and review their development.

The American College Testing Program (2004) also stressed the importance of individual student planning in *Crisis at the Core: Preparing All Students for College and Work*. They recommended that career and educational planning services be provided to all students. In addition, they stated that parents must be involved in key educational and postsecondary planning.

The purpose of the individual student planning program component of the comprehensive guidance and counseling program is to provide all students with guidance and counseling activities to assist them to positively assess, plan for, and then monitor and manage their personal-social, academic, and career development (Cohen, 2001). The point of the activities is to have students focus on their current and future goals by developing life career plans (personal plans of study) drawing on the strengths-based career development content embedded in the guidance curriculum. As Pellitteri et al. (2006) pointed out, "Goals give us our bearing and point us in a purposeful direction" (p. 25). Through the activities of this program component, professional school counselors and others with guidance and counseling responsibilities serve students and parents as facilitators of students' learning of a comprehensive program's strengths-based career development content.

Responsive Services

The holistic focus of our strengths-based career development content allows professional school counselors both a rationale and a set of strategies to meet the social-emotional and personal needs that beset far too many young people. Students who cannot get along with peers or are unable to establish effective relationships with authority figures are not likely to master the ASCA National Standards (ASCA, 2005). Students who lack social skills, are not dependable, and show little initiative are not developing the kinds of strength based work readiness behaviors outlined in our guidance curriculum. Students who have been abused and neglected, or experience crippling problems with anxiety, depression, or anger management are at a great disadvantage in mastering the guidance curriculum strengths that are key to success in school and young adulthood.

This is precisely why professional school counselors are trained to provide effective and up to date counseling intervention to assist these students to overcome personal issues and then be more likely to master the guidance and counseling program's strengths-based content. From this holistic perspective, providing students with responsive services (individual and small group counseling, consultation, and referral services) is a natural part of helping all students develop proactive, resilient, and adaptive approaches to the present and future. For example, professional elementary school counselors who use friendship groups to help students who may be overly shy or aggressive with their peers are helping students to develop the social and prosocial skills that are required for living a successful and satisfied life. These professional elementary counselors are essentially engaged in assisting young people with emotional and behavioral problems to learn and then use sophisticated work readiness behaviors (e.g., listening to another's point of view, being on time, and appropriately standing up for oneself in a group setting), a core content area in our strengths-based guidance curriculum.

Some students require specific assistance to be successful academically, to find purpose and direction in their education, get along with peers and adults, and in setting career goals and in making career choices and plans for the future. They can benefit from individual and small counseling included in responsive services. They can benefit from the opportunity of sharing their thoughts, feelings, and plans individually with school counselors or in small groups with school counselor and other students.

Students may find that the counseling relationship in individual counseling allows them to talk openly and freely about who they are, their present circumstances, and their future plans that they could not do in guidance curriculum and individual student planning activities. They can talk about these issues privately and in confidence. The safety of the counseling relationship allows them to express themselves openly and freely.

Systems Support

Community career partnerships create real world learning contexts that are of great interest to students and a dynamic intervention strategy to assist young people in mastering comprehensive program content standards (Lapan, Osana, Tucker, & Kosciulek, 2002). For example, partnerships funded in the mid-1990s by the School to Work Opportunities Act of 1994 were able to engage young women (especially African American women) in challenging workplace learning contexts and help them to enroll in high school classes that were more focused on their career interests (Hershey, Silverberg, Haimson, Hudis, & Jackson, 1999). Lapan et al. found that business leaders were highly motivated to form such partnerships with their local schools. In chapters 5 and 6, the components of effective community career partnerships will be fully discussed. For now it is important to understand that professional school counselors can use the community outreach aspect of Systems Support to help all students master content standards outlined in our strengths-based guidance curriculum. Professional school counselors can work within the structure of their schools to create programs and activities that connect all community stakeholders (e.g., business leaders, parents, school board members, teachers, and school administrators) in initiatives that create high quality learning experiences for all students.

A Final Note

Comprehensive guidance and counseling programs have a core curriculum like all other instructional programs in our schools. National and state standards provide overarching goals that professional school counselors strive to help all students reach. Grounded in career theory and research, the strengths-based career development content, infused throughout the overall comprehensive guidance and counseling program, focuses professional school counselor efforts on the necessary building blocks of human development that empower all students to be successful in ways outlined by national and state standards. The strengths-based career development content provides a holistic approach that unites the three content domains of an ASCA (2005) recommended comprehensive guidance and counseling program (Academic Development, Career Development, and Personal/Social Development) in a focused and organized effort to help all young people develop proactive, resilient, and adaptive approaches to the present and personally valued futures. Strengths-based career development content is delivered through the four program components of a comprehensive program (Guidance Curriculum, Individual Planning, Responsive Services, and Systems Support; Gysbers & Henderson, 2006). The outcome is that the work of professional school counselors is no longer an ancillary support service in a school because fully implemented comprehensive guidance and counseling programs contribute directly and positively to student success in our schools (Lapan, Gysbers, & Kayson, 2007).

References

America's Career Resource Network. (2006). *National career development guidelines*. Retrieved July 17, 2006, from http://www.acrnetwork.org/ncdg.htm

American College Testing Program. (2004). *Crisis at the core: Preparing all students for college and work*. Iowa City, IA: Author.

American School Counselor Association. (2005). *The ASCA national model: A framework for school counseling programs* (2nd ed.). Alexandria, VA: Author.

Ashcroft, K. B. (1966). *A report of the invitational conference in implementing career development theory*. Washington, DC: National Vocational Guidance Association.

Aubrey, R. F. (1973). A house divided: Guidance and counseling in 20th century America. *Personnel and Guidance Journal, 61*, 198-204.

California State Department of Education. (1971). *Career guidance: A California model for career development K-adult*. Sacramento, CA: Author.

Campbell, C. A., & Dahir, C. A. (1997). *Sharing the vision: The national standards for school counseling programs*. Alexandria, VA: American School Counselor Association.

Cohen, M. (2001). *Transforming the American high school*. Washington, DC: The Aspen Institute.

Davis, J. B. (1914). *Vocational and moral guidance*. Boston: Ginn.

Gysbers, N. C. (1969). *Elements of a model for promoting career development in elementary and junior high school*. Paper presented at the National Conference on Exemplary Programs and Projects, 1968 Amendments to the Vocational Education Act, Atlanta, GA. (ERIC Document Reproduction Service No. ED045860)

Gysbers, N. C. (1985). *Create and use an individual career plan.* Wooster, OH: Bell & Howell Publication Systems Division.

Gysbers, N. C., & Henderson, P. (2006). *Developing and managing your school guidance and counseling program* (4th ed.). Alexandria, VA: American Counseling Association.

Gysbers, N. C., & Moore, E. J. (1974). *Career guidance, counseling and placement: Elements of an illustrative program guide.* Columbia, MO: University of Missouri.

Gysbers, N. C., & Moore, E. J. (1981). *Improving guidance programs.* Englewood Cliffs, NJ: Prentice-Hall.

Gysbers, N. C., Stanley, J. B., Kosteck-Bunch, L., Magnuson, C. S., & Starr, M. F. (2008). *Missouri comprehensive guidance program: A manual for program development, implementation, evaluation and enhancement.* Warrensburg, MO: Missouri Center for Career Education, University of Central Missouri.

Hansen, L. S. (1970). *Career guidance practices in school and community.* Washington, DC: National Vocational Guidance Association.

Herr, E. L. (1969). *Unifying an entire system of education around a career development theme.* Paper presented at the National Conference on Exemplary Programs and Projects, 1968 Amendments to the Vocational Education Act, Atlanta, GA. (ERIC Document Reproduction Service No. ED045860)

Hershey, A. M., Silverberg, M. K., Haimson, J., Hudis, P., & Jackson, R. (1999). *Expanding options for students. Report to Congress on the national evaluation of school-to-work implementation.* Princeton, NJ: Mathematica Policy Research.

Johnson, C. D., & Johnson, S. K. (2001). *Results-based student support programs: Leadership academy workbook.* San Juan Capistrano, CA: Professional Update.

Lapan, R. T., Gysbers, N. C., & Kayson, M. (2007). *Missouri school counselors benefit all students.* Jefferson City, MO: Missouri Department of Elementary and Secondary Education.

Lapan, R. T., Osana, H. P., Tucker, B., & Kosciulek, J. F. (2002). Challenges for creating community career partnerships: Perspectives from practitioners. *The Career Development Quarterly, 51,* 172-190.

Law, B. (2007). *Planning for progression: The future of careers work in the curriculum.* Retrieved October 30, 2008, from http://www.hihohiho.com/magazine/mkngtwork/cafprgrssn.pdf

Missouri School Improvement Program. (2003). *Third-cycle procedures handbook: Revision 5.* Jefferson City, MO: Missouri Department of Elementary and Secondary Education.

Myrick, R. D. (2003). *Developmental guidance and counseling: A practical approach* (4th ed.). Minneapolis, MN: Education Media Corporation.

National Association of Secondary School Principals. (1996). *Breaking ranks: Changing an American institution.* Reston, VA: Author.

National Association of Secondary School Principals. (2004). *Breaking ranks II: Strategies for leading high school reform.* Reston, VA: Author.

National Association of Secondary School Principals. (2006). *Breaking ranks in the middle: Strategies for leading middle level reform.* Reston, VA: Author.

O'Hare, R. W. (1969-70). Evaluation of guidance programs. *California Personnel and Guidance Association Journal, 2,* 5-11.

Orfield, G., & Paul, F. G. (1994). *High hopes long odds: Next steps.* Indianapolis, IN: Indiana Youth Institute.

Parsad, B., Alexander, D., Farris, E., & Hudson, L. (2003). *High school guidance counseling*. Washington, DC: National Center for Educational Statistics, U.S. Department of Education.

Parsons, F. (1909). *Choosing a vocation*. Boston: Houghton Mifflin.

Pellitteri, J., Stern, R., Shelton, C., & Muller-Ackerman, B. (Eds.). (2006). *Emotionally intelligent school counseling*. Mahwah, NJ: Lawrence Erlbaum Associates.

Sprinthall, N. A. (1971). *Guidance for human growth*. New York: Van Nostrand Reinhold.

Squires, D. A. (2005). *Aligning and balancing the standards-based curriculum*. Thousand Oaks, CA: Corwin Press.

Tennyson, W. W., Soldahl, T. A., & Mueller, C. (1965). *The teacher's role in career development*. Washington, DC: National Vocational Guidance Association.

Utah State Board of Education Rules for Comprehensive Guidance Programs, R277-462-3 (1997).

Utah State Statute for Comprehensive Guidance, 53A-17a-131.8 (1996).

Washington State House Bill 2423, (2006). *An act relating to creating a comprehensive guidance, counseling, and planning program in schools.*

Wellman, F. E., & Moore, E. J. (1975). *Pupil personnel services: A handbook for program development and evaluation.* Washington, DC: U.S. Department of Health, Education, and Welfare.

Wiggins, G., & McTighe, J. (1998). *Understanding by design*. Alexandria, VA: Association for Supervision and Curriculum Development.

Wisconsin Department of Public Instruction. (1971). *A K-12 guide for integrating career development into local curriculum.* Madison, WI: Author.

Zins, J. E., Elias, M. J., & Greenberg, M. T. (2007). School practices to build social-emotional competence as the foundation of academic life success. In R. Bar-On, J. G. Maree, & M. J. Elias, *Educating people to be emotionally intelligent* (pp. 79-94). Westport, CN: Praeger.

Chapter 4

Evidence-Based Career Guidance and Counseling Activities in Elementary, Middle, and High Schools

There are three parts to this chapter. Part One discusses the need to develop evidence-based career guidance and counseling practices across the K-12 years that can be implemented in a culturally and contextually competent manner. Part Two provides an overview of some of the leading research that has found significant relationships between student success and career planning interventions. Part Three presents a results-based, developmental model identifying the types of student outcomes likely to be impacted by infusing strengths-based career development content through a comprehensive guidance and counseling program's guidance curriculum, individual student planning, responsive services, and systems support components. The structure of a comprehensive guidance and counseling program is designed to encourage the development and implementation of evidence-based practices. It is fundamentally a results-based framework that encourages professional school counselors to continuously improve their practices to be of greater assistance to all students and their parents.

Part One: Evidence-Based Practices

Dimmitt, Carey, and Hatch (2007) outlined the most far-reaching call to date for professional school counselors to shape their practice around activities and interventions that have credible evidence to support their implementation. When deciding on the interventions to use in order to enhance students' academic, career, and social development, professional school counselors can no longer rely solely on past practice or their "clinical judgment" of what they think is best to do for their students. The National Center for School Counseling Outcome Research (www.umass.edu/schoolcounseling) has since 2002 championed this effort by reviewing research to identify evidence-based and promising practices that would provide a basis for responsible and effective school counseling practices. As pointed out by Dimmitt, Carey, McGannon, and Henningson (2005), evidence-based practices use research evidence to develop effective practices. While promising practices have some research support, they have not yet accumulated the breadth or type of research support necessary to be identified as an evidence-based practice.

The What Works Clearinghouse

The U.S. Department of Education has called for all educational professionals to increase their use of interventions that have been shown to be effective in prior research studies. The Institute for Education Sciences (the research arm of the U.S. Department of Education) has adopted the goal of transforming education into a field where local, state, and national policy and decision makers have sound research and data available to them before recommending interventions or programs that could affect large numbers of students. To empower decision makers with the credible information needed to make better decisions, the Institute for Education Sciences has developed and operates the What Works Clearinghouse (WWC) (http://ies.ed.gov/ncee/wwc).

The WWC strives to improve student outcomes by

identifying educational interventions that work and can be replicated in different school settings. The WWC "collects, screens, and identifies studies of effectiveness of educational interventions (programs, products, practices, and policies)." Relying on the work of Shadish, Cook, and Campbell (2002), the WWC created the Study Design and Implementation Device (Study DIAD). This is a strategy for assessing whether the design and implementation of individual studies allow the researchers to make the claim that there is a causal relationship between an intervention and the intended outcomes of the intervention. The WWC regularly publishes reports on the evidence to support causal relationships between activities and student outcomes.

For example, the WWC published a practice guide for encouraging girls in math and science (Halpern et al., 2007). Practice guidelines collect the best available evidence on problems that can't be addressed in a single approach. In the practice guide to encourage girls in math and science, the WWC makes 5 recommendations and then outlines the level of evidence-based support for each recommendation. First, the WWC recommends that to increase the participation of young women in math and science areas of study, educators should focus on enhancing young women's beliefs about their abilities. They argue that if a young girl sees her abilities in math and science as fixed and unchangeable, then she may be at greater risk to experience discouragement, have lowered performance, and reduce her efforts to master challenges and obstacles. This is clearly covered in the self-efficacy and positive attribution component of our strengths-based career development content model. Second, the WWC encourages educators to provide prescriptive feedback to women about the strategies, effort, and the beliefs they employ to learn math and science content. We would identify this as the self-regulated learning component of our recommended strengths-based career development model. Third, it is recommended that young women be exposed to female role models who have been successful in math and science. Later in this chapter, exposure to role models is identified as a one of the six building blocks of effective evidence-based career practice. Fourth, WWC recommends that teachers create classrooms that spark curiosity and long term interest in math and science. Identifying interests and following one's passions is a fundamental cornerstone of our strengths-based model. And lastly, teachers are encouraged to provide spatial reasoning skills training for young women. Again, we understand this within the self-regulated and lifelong learning component of our strengths-based career development content model.

It is important to note that the WWC recommendations are limited to available experimental or quasi-experimental studies. For example, the evidence supporting the efficacy of exposing young girls to successful female role models was rated as "Low." This is due to the fact that the WWC only had a few small experimental studies of college women available to them. They did not have studies looking at the effects for K-12 students. It is important to realize that while the WWC supports the validity of multiple approaches (e.g., qualitative methods), to date they have focused their attention only on studies that employ experimental and quasi-experimental designs.

This is a major limitation of their work. In the case of the "Low" evidence rating for math and science role models for young girls, the WWC does not have credible experimental studies to make a determination of the effectiveness or lack of effectiveness of exposing young women to successful role models. This fact is included in the text explaining this rating in the practice guide. Professional school counselors and other career development professionals using WWC information should keep this clearly in mind when evaluating the validity and

utility of the recommendations made by this valuable Department
of Education service.

National Panel for Evidence-Based School Counseling

The WWC has developed a very rigorous and extensive
set of criteria to assess whether or not the methods used in a
particular study could establish a causal relationship between an
intervention and intended student outcomes (see the WWC's
Study DIAD). It was clear that this intricate set of evaluative
measurements would be too time consuming and impractical for
use by professional school counselors. What was needed was a
smaller subset of critical benchmarks professional school
counselors could use to assess the adequacy of the interventions
they were currently using or were planning to adopt.

The National Center for School Counseling Outcome
Research convened a panel of leading counselor educators to
develop a practical but scientifically defensible set of domains
that professional school counselors could use to determine the
level of evidence an intervention possessed to support its claim
that it could promote positive change in critical student outcomes.
This work resulted in the development of seven domains that
professional school counselors could use to determine the
evidence-based status of any intervention they were considering
implementing with students. Table 4-1 describes each of the
seven domains (Measurement, Comparison Groups, Statistical
Analysis of Outcome Variables, Implementation Fidelity,
Replication, Ecological Validity, and Persistence of Effect) that
the Panel evaluated at two different levels of strength (i.e., Strong
Evidence and Promising Evidence). For example, the domain of
Measurement focuses attention on the reliability and validity of
the instruments (e.g., pretest or posttest measures) used to assess
change associated with the intervention. An intervention would

Table 4-1: Criteria developed by the National Panel for Evidence-Based School Counseling

National Panel for School Counseling Evidence-Based Practice

Outcome Research Coding Protocol

School counseling interventions will be evaluated by the Evidence-Based Practice Panel to determine the level of evidence that exists in outcome studies that supports the contention that the intervention causes a change in an important student outcome. Seven domains will be used in this evaluation and each domain has threshold criteria for two levels of strength: strong evidence and promising evidence. To be considered an evidence-based practice, an intervention must exceed the strong evidence threshold in all seven areas. To be considered promising practice, an intervention must exceed the promising evidence threshold in all seven areas.

Three Panel members will independently review the outcome research related to a given intervention and independently rate each intervention on all seven criteria. Consensus in ratings will be achieved through consultation. The panel will disseminate its overall rating and, in cases where interventions fail to achieve evidence-based practice or promising practice status, an analysis of deficiencies in the evidence base will be offered.

The seven domains and criteria are included below:

Domain 1. Measurement
Principle: Important academic, career and/or personal/social outcomes are measured using reliable and valid instruments.
Strong Evidence:
1. Outcomes measures have established high reliability and validity characteristics.
2. Outcome measures are established to be appropriate for the population under study.
Promising Evidence:
1. Reliability characteristics are evaluated in the study and show adequate reliability.
2. Logical argument supports the appropriateness of the measures for the population under study.

Domain 2. Comparison Groups
Principle: Comparison groups with adequate controls are included so that resulting group differences can be attributed to the intervention.
Strong Evidence:
1. Active comparison groups (alternative treatment) with adequate controls (attention, placebo) are included in an outcome study.
2. Initial group equivalence is assured through random assignment.
3. Group equivalence in mortality/attrition is established.
Promising Evidence:
1. Groups equated through matching or statistical procedures (e.g. ANOVA) or strong pre/post-test designs are used with adequate controls.

Domain 3. Statistical Analyses of Outcome Variables
Principle: Statistical analysis documents low probability of Type 1 error and potency of intervention.

Strong Evidence:
1. Statistically significant finding using appropriate test.
2. Control for experiment-wise error rate.
3. Adequate N (number of participants in study).
4. At least a moderate effect size for critical outcome variables.

Promising Evidence:
1. Statistically significant finding using appropriate test.
2. Control for experiment-wise error rate.
3. Adequate N.
4. At least a small effect size for critical outcome variables.

Domain 4. Implementation Fidelity

Principle: Intervention can be delivered with fidelity across contexts and is not contaminated by implementer.

Strong Evidence:
1. Intervention is extensively documented (manual or protocol) so that it can be reliably replicated.
2. Intervention is delivered by multiple people with adequate training and checks for adherence to protocol.

Promising Evidence:
1. Intervention is standardized and can be delivered across contexts.
2. Intervention is delivered by multiple people with adequate training.

Domain 5. Replication

Principle: The same intervention independently implemented with an equivalent population results in equivalent outcomes.

Strong Evidence:
1. Independent evaluators find equivalent outcomes with a similar population.

Promising Evidence:
1. Same evaluator finds equivalent outcomes with same population.

Domain 6. Ecological Validity

Principle: The intervention can be implemented effectively in a public school with consistent effects across all student subgroups or with known differences between student subgroups. Limitations of the generalizability of results are clearly explicated.

Strong Evidence:
1. Study conducted in a diverse public school.
2. Outcomes are assessed across different subgroups of students or clearly specified as valid for a specific subgroup.

Promising Evidence:
1. Study conducted in a private, laboratory, or charter school or in a public school with limited diversity.

Domain 7. Persistence of Effect

Principle: The intervention results in a lasting effect on an important outcome measure.

Strong Evidence:
1. Treatment-comparison group differences are demonstrated to persist for a practically significant time period.

Promising Evidence:
1. Treatment-comparison group differences are demonstrated to persist beyond the immediate implementation.

be rated as having "Strong Evidence" if the measures used to assess change had clearly established reliability and validity and the measures were appropriate for the intended student population. If the study or intervention did not meet this high standard, it could be rated as having "Promising Evidence" if the measures had been successfully used in previous study, had adequate reliability, and a logical argument could be made that the measures were appropriate for use with the particular student groups of interest to professional school counselors.

The National Panel agreed that to earn a rating as an "Evidence-Based Practice" an intervention had to demonstrate "Strong Evidence" on each of the seven domains. To earn a rating as a "Promising Practice," an intervention would have to demonstrate at least "Promising Evidence" on each of the seven domains. The work of the National Panel was first presented at the 2005 ASCA National Convention (Carey et al., 2005). The first publication based on the Panel's work has been published in *Professional School Counseling* (Carey, Dimmitt, Hatch, Lapan, Lee, & Whiston, 2008). While the impetus to develop this set of standards was in part motivated by the scarcity of well controlled studies in school counseling (Whiston, Sexton, & Lasoff, 1998), professional school counselors can employ the Panel's evaluation framework to assess the adequacy of the activities and interventions that they are planning to implement in their schools.

Professional counselors can use the seven domains of the National Panel for Evidence-Based School Counseling when deciding on the specific career development activities and interventions to use in their schools. For example, there are career assessments available for purchase where students answer a very short list of Likert items. From these scant few items, students are provided feedback on their personality, work values, and interests. Educational professionals should quickly challenge the reliability and validity of this kind of measurement strategy and not allow students to stereotype themselves based on this inadequate measurement strategy. As well, if there is no reasonable comparison group then it is impossible to attribute positive change to the intervention. Advertisers who extol the virtue of their intervention may be doing so based on studies where they have not provided the activity to enough students and then have conducted too many statistical tests on these few students.

Practices such as this violate basic statistical assumptions (e.g., Type I error) and exploit chance correlations in their inadequate samples. If there is no documentation of how to carry out an intervention or no evidence that it has been done by others, professional school counselors and other career professionals should pause to consider whether or not they will be able to successfully carry out the set of activities with enough fidelity to achieve the intended outcomes for students. And finally, if an intervention has not been replicated, there is doubt about the feasibility of doing it in a public school, or it is unlikely the treatment effects will last for a reasonable amount of time (e.g., three to six months), then professional school counselors need to be very clear about why they are doing this intervention and cautious because of the lack of an evidence base to support it.

Six Building Blocks of Evidence-Based Career Practices

When designing activities to carry out a strengths-based guidance curriculum that has some evidence to back it up, professional counselors should keep the 3 Cs clearly in mind (i.e., common factors, culture, and context). Common factors have been found to explain approximately 70% of the benefits that people get from receiving psychotherapy and counseling services (Wampold, 2001). Refuting the claims that specific treatments are needed for specific disorders (e.g., a cognitive-behavioral intervention for a problem with anxiety or depression), Wampold found that factors common to all treatments determine the effectiveness of any single intervention (e.g., creating a working alliance with the client where they can deal with overwhelming and alienating feelings, instilling a sense of hopefulness for the client, creating a healing context, providing a believable explanation to the client for their problems, and engaging clients in rituals and practices connected to this believable explanation; Frank & Frank, 1991).

Wampold went on to say that counseling is fundamentally a healing process anchored in layers of culture and context. To be effective, believable explanations and treatment practices must be congruent with the cultural and contextual beliefs and values of the client. The worldview of the person seeking help is an essential ingredient in any effective intervention. In addition, Shadish et al. (2002) concluded that all causes are context dependent. As qualitative researchers have been quick to point out, lifting presumed causes out of the cultural contexts in which they were presumably implemented and generalizing this finding as a causal relationship applicable to other times, places, and persons is an undertaking fraught with error and misinterpretation. For a more complete discussion of how to provide culturally and contextually competent career counseling, see Lapan (2004), as well as leading writers on diversity and counseling (e.g., Lee, 1997; and Sue & Sue, 2008).

Herr and Cramer (1972) encouraged researchers to focus on how, why, for whom, and under what conditions career guidance and counseling interventions could be effective. Recent work is beginning to shed light on the common factors in career guidance and counseling that lead to enhanced career outcomes (Ryan, 1999). In a meta-analytic review of the research, five factors were found to have a positive relationship to treatment outcomes. Very much in sync with the findings from Wampold's contextual model of counseling, five common factors have been identified that improve career outcomes for students or career clients (Brown & Krane, 2000). Below, each is listed as one of the building blocks of evidence-based career practices. Given the research just cited, a sixth common factor directly related to culture, context, and diversity has been added. We are suggesting these as starting points for professional counselors developing a strengths-based comprehensive guidance and counseling program. While additional features can be added to enrich any intervention, professional counselors designing an evidence-based career intervention should at the very least begin by including each of these six building blocks (i.e., common factors) of effective practice. In Chapter 6, you will be provided with a way to do a curriculum audit assessing how well these building blocks are incorporated into the strengths-based comprehensive guidance and counseling program in your school building.

1. <u>Build relationships with students</u>
   By far and away the best strategy to help young people achieve the objectives of a strengths-based guidance and counseling program is to establish a working alliance with them (Bordin, 1979; Meara & Patton, 1994). Agreement on the tasks to be accomplished, the goals to be reached, and the emotional bonds that tie students and counselors together will enable career professionals to be influential in the lives of young people. More effective career interventions provide young people the opportunity for one-on-one interaction and feedback related to any assessment results. In the context of having a meaningful relationship with a professional counselor, students will become more deeply engaged in exploring possible future

educational and career options and in setting challenging but attainable goals.

2. <u>Build emotional and instrumental support for students in their immediate environments</u>

Young people need emotional and instrumental support from the important people and contexts in their lives to successfully move towards realizing their educational and career dreams. In addition to what professional school counselors can do, support from peers, teachers, and parents is vital. Parent involvement may be one of the most neglected areas of a school-based career intervention. For strategies on how to include parents in strengths-based career development interventions, see Lapan (2008).

3. <u>Build relationships between students and role models</u>

Exposing students to role models they can identify with and want to be like is an important component of an effective intervention. Role models inspire students and provide them invaluable career information.

4. <u>Build student understanding with accurate and up to date information about postsecondary options and the world of work</u>

Students need user-friendly information that helps them to better understand the world of work and their place in it. Freely available Internet resources like O*NET (www.onetcenter.org) make this possible for any strengths-based intervention.

5. <u>Build commitment of students to follow through on their decisions and plans</u>

Brown and Krane (2000) found that having career clients write down their thoughts, feelings, and self-reflections had a small but statistically significant relationship with improved outcomes. Journals, logs, diaries, and workbooks can engage students in the career exploration process. Writing and signing a contract can help to build a commitment to follow through on the goals and plans they are creating.

6. <u>Build culturally and contextually competent activities, interventions, and programs</u>

Any effective career intervention must address all the relevant issues related to human diversity. Critical stakeholders (e.g., students, parents, community leaders, and local business leaders) need to be at the table to ensure that culture, context, and setting are adequately addressed in every aspect of a strengths-based career curriculum. For example, professional counselors could establish an advisory council to make sure that this value is infused into every activity that is undertaken.

Part Two:
What Is the Relationship Between Career Guidance and Counseling Activities and Student Success?

Career guidance and counseling student planning activities can have a considerable positive impact on student success across the K-12 school years. Beginning at least in the 1950s and continuing through to the present, there is credible research and scholarship to make the plausible argument that helping young people to explore and plan for their short and long term futures can have the added beneficial result of enhancing their academic achievement and career development as well as social/emotional growth. While for a number of reasons (e.g., lack of available grant funding and the immense difficulties of conducting randomized control group studies in public school settings) the definitive studies have not yet been completed, we feel that there is enough evidence to at least designate certain career interventions as "Promising Practices."

Employing the standards established by the National Panel for Evidence-Based School Counseling, there is "Promising Evidence" that student success has been enhanced by interventions that have: 1) used reliable measurements across several studies that are logically appropriate for use with K-12 student populations; 2) employed comparison groups that approximate the treatment groups by using appropriate matching and statistical controls; 3) had adequate sample size, calculated appropriate statistical tests, and attained effect sizes important in real world contexts; 4) been successfully delivered by different people, in different school contexts, and in a manner that maintained fidelity to the original intervention; 5) replicated their findings with similar student populations; 6) been shown to be practical for use in public school settings; and 7) been shown to be of help to students for a reasonable time period after the intervention ended.

Shadish et al. (2002) have written what many leading experts consider the most definitive statement on experimental and quasi-experimental design for use in educational and social science research. The Institute for Education Sciences relied heavily on this work to develop the Study DIAD now utilized by the WWC. Even a casual review of this text reveals the dilemmas and ambiguities involved in any attempt to establish a causal relationship between treatments and outcomes. Like Galileo using a telescope to establish that the earth moves around the sun, we use observational methods to try and understand how the world around us works. Evidence-based approaches are not content to live off outdated theories and dogma. To learn the secrets of phenomena critical to our field, we must as Francis Bacon said "twist the lion's tail" and see what happens.

Unfortunately, all of our ways of seeing are flawed. Leading quantitative and qualitative methods have enormous strengths, while at the same time they are wrought through and through with glaring defects. For example, Shadish et al. (2002) pointed out that to understand why an intervention works, researchers need to use qualitative methods. This information is not something that can be obtained from available quasi-experimental procedures. Truly randomized studies are enormously expensive and difficult to do in public school settings. And even if this were not the case, the more that researchers tighten up on the internal validity of their study (i.e., imposing controls that lead to a highly probable argument that a specific event caused a measurable change), they then run the risk of reducing the external validity of their work (i.e., they may hurt the generalizability of their findings).

There is no one right way to gather the credible information we need. To understand constructs of critical importance to our field (e.g., student success), we need to rely on multiple methods and different ways of knowing (e.g., qualitative methods and action research). Each of the observational research methods currently available provides unique vantage points to investigate the human condition. However, upon closer inspection, each method also has significant shortcomings.

Shadish et al. (2002) suggested that in the untidy world of education, social science research, and human relations, we seek credible information to make plausible arguments about the relationships between causes and effects. For example, several studies have found that there is a curvilinear relationship between the number of hours adolescents work in part time jobs and their grades. That is to say, like the relationship between stress and performance, a few hours of working in a part time job may actually lead to better grades. However, at a certain point the trend line reverses itself and the more an adolescent works in a part time job, the worse their grades are likely to become (see Lapan, 2004 for a review of the research on adolescent career development).

The Terman longitudinal study of high gifted women in the first half of the 20th century found that women with exceptionally high IQs who did not use their talents outside of their homemaker roles were at greater risk for suffering from depression and being dissatisfied with their lives (Sears & Barbie, 1977). Should we discount research like this and the relationship between hours worked and adolescents' grades because they did not employ randomized or quasi-experimental procedures? We would say no. Instead, we would argue that there is credible information from many reputable sources that have used a variety of respected research tools (e.g., correlational methods, multiple regression analyses, structural equation modeling, quasi-experimental approaches, and qualitative studies) to make the plausible argument that career development and educational planning can have a meaningful and substantial impact on student success. A brief discussion of some of this credible information is provided below.

Our Profession's History

Unfortunately, many practitioners and policy makers are not aware of the highly credible research legacy that comes down to us today from early visionaries in school guidance and counseling (see Gysbers, 2004 for a full review of research beginning in the 1920s). For example, in the 1950s and 1960s several academics (whom today we would call counselor educators) championed the idea of providing all K-12 students the benefit of having a professional school counselor. These early pioneers argued that it was worth the cost to hire professional school counselors because substantial benefits would accrue to students as they transitioned into young adulthood, if they had the opportunity to work with a trained counselor. Not content to merely proclaim this to be true, several tested this hypothesis by conducting longitudinal studies that still stand today for the rigor and quality with which they were completed. The best would be the work conducted in the state of Wisconsin by John Rothney.

Rothney (1958) followed a group of 690 sophomores for five years after they graduated from high school. Selecting a random sample of students from four different high schools, Rothney created a quasi-experimental study that compared a group of students receiving counseling services to a control group of students who did not receive counseling. With dogged determination, he followed these young people as they transitioned into young adulthood. Rothney's efforts can be seen in the extremely small number of missing cases that he could not account for and provide data.

The findings from this study were striking. Those students who received counseling services while in high school experienced better outcomes in young adulthood on a number of dimensions that are of central concern to this day. For example, students receiving counseling services in high school: a) had slightly better high school grades; b) were more likely to enter post-secondary education; and c) were more likely to graduate from this post-secondary training. In addition, students receiving guidance services: a) were more consistent with their vocational choices; b) remained longer in their chosen areas of employment; and c) made more progress in their work. These individuals reported greater satisfaction with their lives five years after graduating from high school. They felt more satisfied with their high school experiences and the counseling they received.

Rothney's findings strike at the core of several key

initiatives and ideas that would later blossom as fundamental concerns and societal directives. For example, Rothney's work connects to ideas and initiatives such as the School-to-Work Opportunities Act of 1994, Donald Super's call to help adolescents transition into more stabilized career paths in young adulthood, and positive psychology's emphasis on constructs such as happiness and well being. The School-to-Work Opportunities Act of 1994 specifically focused on how schools could help young people more effectively transition into young adulthood. Well over a billion dollars was spent to develop local responses to this critical challenge. Unfortunately, organized and systematic comprehensive guidance and counseling programs were not a focus of this legislation. Rothney's work suggests that career guidance and counseling efforts in high school can lead to improved student success both while they are in high school and when they transition into young adulthood. For such national initiatives to be successful, strenghts-based comprehensive guidance and counseling programs need to be at the heart of the effort.

Credible Evaluation Studies Not Completed for Publication in Peer Refereed Journals

The time honored peer-review process in counseling and development has published a number of high quality studies that support the relationship between career exploration and planning activities and student success. Two meta-analyses summarized the results across these studies and argued for meaningful relationships (Baker & Taylor, 1998; Evans & Burck, 1992). For example, Evans and Burck found the largest effects between career development activities and student academic achievement occurred during the elementary school years. While further work certainly needs to be done before any definitive conclusions can be drawn, findings consistently support that making student learning relevant to possible career futures is a good thing for students.

Recently, a new body of credible information is beginning to take shape. This is work done as part of independent, external evaluations of career development interventions. The authors of these studies are often highly competent researchers, who are carrying out their evaluation work not for the purposes of publication in peer-refereed journals. Unfortunately, results are then published only online and do not become part of the peer-reviewed body of knowledge. While readers need to be careful of the rigor of these studies, already several have much to say about the relationship between effective career interventions and student success. We would recommend readers use the seven criteria established by the National Panel for Evidence-Based School Counseling to assess the validity of these evaluation studies. They are certainly not without flaws. However, there is very credible work now coming available on the Internet that adds to our understanding. Three examples are provided below.

Utah has financial support through their state legislature to have professional school counselors implement comprehensive guidance and counseling programs. The heart of this program is organized around the Student Education and Occupation Plan (SEOP). Interventions include structured guidance curriculum across Grades 6 through 12, and Individual Planning activities that mandate at least annual meetings between students, parents, and fully trained school counselors. See the description of this comprehensive program that is being implemented in the Granite School District in Salt Lake City (www.graniteschools.org).

Nelson and Gardner (1998), an independent evaluation company, were commissioned to study the impact on Utah students attending schools that had more fully implemented this comprehensive program. Some of the more provocative findings included the following. Students attending high schools with this comprehensive guidance and counseling program in place scored higher on every subtest of the ACT than students attending high schools that were not providing these services. Students in high implementing schools were more likely to meet with their parents and school counselors to plan their educational courses of studies. These students were also more likely to both enroll in and pass more advanced math and science courses. These students enrolled in more career and technical education courses. And finally, they were much more satisfied with the guidance and career planning services they were receiving in their schools.

In 2007 another study was completed concerning the nature and impact of Utah's Comprehensive Guidance and Counseling Program (Nelson, Fox, Haslam, & Gardner, 2007). The findings of the 2007 study substantiated the findings of the 1998 study. For example, students in high implementing schools took greater numbers of higher-level English, mathematics, and technology oriented courses, attained higher levels of academic achievement, and made better decisions about education and career planning than students attending lower-implementing schools.

The state of Washington has now developed and is implementing a comprehensive guidance and career counseling program called "Navigation 101" (www.k12.wa.us/navigation 101). There are 5 key components to this program (i.e., small group curriculum driven advisories that involve all the educational professionals in a school, portfolios, student led conferences that include parents, student driven scheduling, and program evaluation). The Washington State University Social and Economic Sciences Research Center conducted an extensive evaluation of Navigation 101 (2007). Among other important outcomes, they found that students attending schools that had implemented this organized and extensive approach to career and education planning: a) were more likely to take and pass "gatekeeper" courses like Algebra, Physics, and Chemistry; b) had higher 10th grade state achievement test scores; c) were less likely to drop out of school as they moved from 9th to 10th grade; d) were more likely to graduate from high school; e) had more parents participating in education and career planning conferences; and f) were less likely to need remedial courses when entering community college programs. Approximately 52% of Washington students required remedial coursework to be successful at the community colleges they entered. Navigation 101 schools saw a significant reduction in their graduates needing remedial courses.

And finally, the private company Mathematica was hired by the federal government to evaluate the impact of the School-to-Work Opportunities Act of 1994. Mathematica's report to Congress in 1999 clearly identified tangible benefits for students participating in schools that were offering the three components of this federal legislation (i.e., school-based learning, work-based learning, and connecting activities). Among other findings, Hershey et al. (1999) argued that: a) women, especially African American women, highly valued these learning opportunities and were more likely to participate in work-based learning experiences; b) high academically achieving and low academically achieving students were equally likely to participate in school-to-work learning opportunities; c) students intending to go to 4-year colleges were now more likely to take courses that they saw as being more relevant and related to their career goals; d) non-college bound students' participation in courses related to their career goals had nearly doubled from the 1996 baseline; and e) many more students were taking classes directly related to their career interests, especially in schools with large African American student populations.

The Present and the Future

There is reputable scholarship both within and outside of

the fields of school guidance and counseling and career development to suggest a strong link to student success. This is likely to be refined, elaborated, and expanded upon in the future with the now combined use of mixed analytic methods (e.g., path analysis, qualitative narrative methods, and action research). For example, Schneider and Stevenson (1999) conducted a rigorous qualitative study of adolescent educational and career aspirations for the Alfred P. Sloan Foundation. They concluded that high schools that didn't provide educational and career planning services had students with "misaligned ambitions." These students exhibited a profound mismatch between the amount of education they expected to attain and the education actually required for the career they expected to enter. However, in those high schools that emphasized career and educational planning, students exhibited more personal agency and were taking more responsibility for the educational decisions they were making. Schneider and Stevenson described the most effective high schools in their sample. The effective elements they identified are the essential components of what Gysbers & Henderson (2006) have long recommended as being central to comprehensive guidance and counseling programs.

The Achieving Success Identity Pathways program (Howard & Solberg, 2006) has shown very promising results in enhancing student success through a career development approach. This classroom guidance curriculum intervention has been implemented and evaluated with over 2,500, 9th through 12th graders. While this work is mostly correlational in nature and lacks adequate control groups, promising changes have been found in student grades, credits earned, school attendance, reduction in school suspensions, and improvement in anger management. Future quasi-experimental studies could employ needed control groups to further substantiate benefits that accrue to students who participate in this program.

Career development planning and explorations has also been found to enhance student academic engagement. Kenny, Blustein, Haase, Jackson, and Perry (2006) studied the relationship between career planfulness and student engagement in school (i.e., feelings of belonging and valuing of school) in a multi-ethnic study of urban 9th graders. Findings supported the hypothesis that career planfulness was a positive contributor to student engagement across the school year for these 9th graders. Studies such as this lay the evidentiary basis to establish career development activities as a useful and necessary component in any educational reform effort that seeks to enhance student success.

Several studies have been conducted in Missouri to investigate the relationship between career development and student success. Four of these studies are briefly noted below. In a statewide study of approximately 23,000 high school students, Lapan, Gysbers, and Sun (1997) found that students in schools implementing a comprehensive guidance and counseling program reported that their schools were making more career and college information available to them. These students felt that their high schools were doing a better job preparing them for the future. Second, when evaluating a guidance curriculum unit co-taught between language arts teachers and school counselors, Lapan, Gysbers, Hughey, and Arni (1993) found a significant link between academic achievement (i.e., grades based on grammar and writing skills displayed on a major research paper) and growth in the kinds of career development skills comprehensive programs promote. Third, in a three-year longitudinal study of rural 12th graders, Lapan, Aoyagi, and Kayson (2007) found that seniors who had organized their high school studies around a meaningful career goal were further along in mastering the career development competencies recommended by the Integrative/

Contextual Model of Career Development (Lapan, 2004). Seniors with these career development advantages were more likely three-years after graduating from high school to have attended postsecondary educational training, experienced greater success in transitioning into the worker role, and reported greater satisfaction with the overall quality of their lives.

And finally, Lapan, Gysbers, and Kayson (2007) completed a statewide study in Missouri examining the benefits for all students when a comprehensive program is implemented (www.missouricareereducation.org). Figure 4-1 presents a pie chart depicting the hierarchical multiple regression results to answer the research question of whether or not there is a relationship between a high school's ability to meet the adequate yearly progress (AYP) requirements of No Child Left Behind and the educational and career planning services provided in that high school. After statistically removing the effects on AYP due to 4 prominent factors (1. the fact that some schools spend considerably more money per student than other schools; 2. the effects on academic achievement related to the enrollment size of the school; 3. the impact on school-level student achievement related to the percentage of students receiving free and reduced lunch; and 4. the fact that there are significant differences between schools related to the ratios between classroom teachers and students, as well as the training and experience level of teachers), those high schools that were doing a better job providing their students with educational and career planning services were also doing a better job meeting AYP. Career planning uniquely explained 3% of the variance after these other four factors were taken into account. From all of these sources (e.g., our professional history, current evaluation studies, and available quantitative and qualitative research), we would argue that there already exists credible information to make the plausible argument that the strengths-based career curriculum proposed in this book does promote student success.

Part Three: A Results-Based Model

Figure 4-1

Question: Do educational and career planning activities help high schools to meet the AYP (adequate yearly progress) requirements of No Child Left Behind? Answer: Yes!

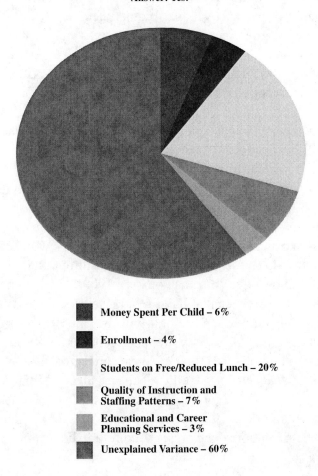

Money Spent Per Child – 6%

Enrollment – 4%

Students on Free/Reduced Lunch – 20%

Quality of Instruction and Staffing Patterns – 7%

Educational and Career Planning Services – 3%

Unexplained Variance – 60%

Figure 4-2 presents a results-based model identifying the types of outcomes that can be positively impacted by implementing a strengths-based guidance and counseling program. Four interconnected sets of outcomes measure advantages to students who attend schools that have more fully implemented programs. Benefits accrue to students as they progress through the K-12 years, prepare to transition to postsecondary education and training, and eventually find success and well being across the critical network of life roles in adulthood. This model is fully consistent with the longstanding perspective that comprehensive guidance and counseling programs are results-based systems that constantly seek to improve benefits to students in measurable ways (e.g., Johnson & Johnson, 1982; Lapan, 2001; Mitchell & Gysbers, 1978).

Interventions that are designed to incorporate the six building blocks of evidence-based practice will be more likely to promote the behavioral targets of the integrative/contextual model of career development (Lapan, 2004). For example, interventions that build student understanding of the world of work through accurate and up to date information will be more likely to help students grow in the person-environment fit component of the strengths-based curriculum. These students will have an advantage in terms of better understanding themselves and the world of work, and how to do the "true reasoning" that will optimally connect these two knowledge domains (Parsons, 1909). In addition, career development activities that build relationships with students and professional school counselors will be more successful in motivating students to explore postsecondary education and training options and in setting effective career goals.

Students who master these behavioral targets will be more likely to attain critical formative outcomes during the K-12 years. That is to say they will internalize a proactive, resilient, and adaptive orientation to the present and future. For example, these

Figure 4-2

Developmental Outcomes Enhanced by Evidence-Based Career Guidance and Counseling Interventions

Evidence-Based Interventions

Six building blocks of effective interventions:
1. Relationships
2. Support
3. Role Model
4. Information
5. Commitment
6. Cultural and contextual competence

Targets of the Intervention

1. Self-efficacy beliefs
2. Goal formation and exploration skills
3. Knowledge of self and the world of work, and how they fit together
4. Career interests
5. Effective, self-regulated learners
6. Work readiness behaviors and social skills

Formative Outcomes

Engage students in their school activities, helping them to feel that they belong and are more deeply connected to their learning. This engagement, sense of belonging, and connectedness is related to the strengthening of a proactive, resilient, and adaptive orientation to the present and future that is characterized by growth in:
Purpose and Direction
Opportunity and Choice
Agency and Empowerment
Commitment and Maturity
Motivation and Hopefulness
Perseverance and an ability to overcome Obstacles
Creativity and Curiosity
Entrepreneurship and a Caring for Others and the Environment

Summative Markers of K-12 School Success

For example:
Development of a personally meaningful, autonomously chosen career plan
GPA, Test scores, and Graduation rates
Attendance and behavior in school
Relationships with teachers
Course selection patterns
Leadership roles performed in school
Participation in school and after school activities, e.g., clubs and related school sponsored opportunities

Readiness to make Successful Postsecondary Transitions

1. Personal Development
2. Effective student and lifelong learner
3. Age appropriate and mature commitment to pursue Postsecondary Education and Career Pathway
4. Diversity Skills

Satisfaction, Well Being, and Success in Adult Life Roles

1. Worker
2. Learner
3. Citizen and Community Member
4. Spousal Partner
5. Global Citizen
6. Personal well being
7. Leisurite

117

young people will be more likely to develop a sense of purpose, direction, and meaning in their engagement in the present and movement towards desired futures. They will be both more motivated and hopeful. They will see choices for themselves, be able to persevere to overcome obstacles, be curious, make mature commitments to their education and training, and be willing to display empathy for others and safeguard the environments we need to survive.

Students who realize these formative outcomes in their lives will be more likely to display outcomes consistently identified as indicating success during the K-12 school years (i.e., Summative Markers of K-12 School Success). These young people will be able to develop autonomously chosen career plans. Their Grade Point Average, test scores, graduation rates, attendance, and behavior in school will be better than students who do not master these formative outcomes. These students will be more likely to fill leadership roles and participate in school activities. The K-12 summative outcomes listed in Figure 4-2 are not meant to be an exhaustive list. We believe that they are the types of summative outcomes that will be positively enhanced by participation in a strengths-based guidance and counseling program.

Students who meet these summative markers of K-12 success will be better prepared to make successful transitions to postsecondary education and training. Given the incredibly high failure rates that accompany many students when they begin their postsecondary education, it is critical that students have realized these summative outcomes before they graduate from high school. If they have, these young people will have the personal development necessary to successfully cope with the transition out of high school. They will have successfully demonstrated their skills at being a self-regulated learner. They will be making age appropriate commitments to a postsecondary direction that matches their maturing understanding of themselves. These young people will have learned the diversity skills needed to one day be a global citizen. In short, as Super, Savickas, and Super (1996) suggested, these high school seniors will have internalized the set of skills and attitudes that will increase the likelihood that they will find success and satisfaction in young adulthood.

And finally, young people who make more successful transitions into postsecondary education and training will be more likely to realize success and satisfaction in young adulthood. They will find career directions that are personally meaningful and rewarding. They will graduate from postsecondary settings. They will become responsible citizens, community members, and spousal partners. Global citizenship will be within their reach, as well as an enhanced sense of personal well being. The long term outcome of evidence-based practices that help students master the objectives of strengths-based career development content embedded in comprehensive guidance and counseling programs is to provide young people adaptive advantages as they transition into adulthood.

In Summary

This chapter presented a framework professional counselors can use to develop evidence-based career activities, interventions, and programs. Educational professionals can utilize the assessment tool developed by the National Panel for Evidence-Based School Counseling to determine the strengths and weaknesses of any career intervention they might want to implement with their students. By designing career activities around the six building blocks of evidence-based career practice, professional school counselors are more likely to help all of their students realize the objectives of the strengths-based career development content embedded in a comprehensive guidance and counseling program. A brief review of the research was offered suggesting that a considerable relationship exists between evidence-based career interventions and student success. And finally, a results-based model was described that assists professional school counselors in identifying the types of short and long term career development outcomes enhanced by participation in comprehensive guidance and counseling programs.

References

Baker, S. B., & Taylor, J. G. (1998). Effects of career education interventions: A meta-analysis. *Career Development Quarterly, 46*(4), 376-385.

Bordin, E. S. (1979). The generalizability of the psychoanalytic concept of the working alliance. *Psychotherapy, Research, and Practice, 16*, 252-260.

Brown, S. D., & Krane, N. E. (2000). Four (or five) sessions and a cloud of dust: Old assumptions and new observations about career counseling. In S. D. Brown & R. W. Lent (Eds.), *Handbook of counseling psychology* (3rd ed., pp. 740-766). New York: Wiley.

Carey, J., Dimmit, C., Hatch, T., Lapan, R. T., Lee, C., & Whiston, S. (2005, July). *Second annual report of the National Panel for evidence-based school counseling interventions.* Presented at the annual convention of the American School Counselor Association.

Carey, J. C., Dimmitt, C., Hatch, T., Lapan, R. T., & Whiston, S.C. (2008). Report of the national panel for evidence-based school counseling: Outcome research coding protocol and evaluation of student success skills and second step. *Professional School Counselor, 11(3)*, 197-206.

Dimmitt, C. L., Carey, J. C., & Hatch, P. A. (2007). *Evidence-based school counseling: Making a difference with data-driven practices.* Thousand Oaks, CA: Corwin Press.

Dimmitt, C. L., Carey, J.C., McGannon, W., & Henningson, I. (2005). Identifying a school counseling research agenda: A Delphi study. *Counselor Education and Supervision, 44*, 214-228.

Evans, J. H., & Burck, H. D. (1992). The effects of career education interventions on academic achievement: A meta-analysis. *Journal of Counseling and Development, 71*(1), 63-68.

Frank, J. D., & Frank, J. B. (1991). *Persuasion and healing: A comparative study of psychotherapy* (3rd ed.). Baltimore: Johns Hopkins University Press.

Gysbers, N. C. (2004). Comprehensive guidance and counseling programs: The evolution of accountability. *Professional School Counseling, 8*, 1-14.

Gysbers, N. C., & Henderson, P. (2006). *Developing and managing your school guidance and counseling program* (4th ed.). Alexandria, VA: American Counseling Association.

Halpern, D., Aronson, J., Reimer, N., Simpkins, S., Star, J., & Wentzel, K. (2007). *Encouraging girls in math and science* (NCER 2007-2003). Washington, DC: National Center for Education Research, Institute of Education Sciences, U.S. Department of Education.

Herr, E. L., & Cramer, S. H. (1972). *Vocational guidance and career development in the schools: Toward a systems approach*. Boston: Houghton Mifflin.

Hershey, A. M., Silverberg, M. K., Haimson, J., Hudis, P., & Jackson, R. (1999). *Expanding options for students. Report to Congress on the National Evaluation of School-to-Work Implementation*. Princeton, NJ: Mathematica Policy Research.

Howard, K. A. S., & Solberg, V. S. H. (2006). School-based social justice: The achieving success identity pathways program. *Professional School Counseling, 9*, 278-287

Johnson, C. D., & Johnson, S. K. (1982). Competency based training of career development specialists or "let's get off the calf path." *Vocational Guidance Quarterly, 32*, 327-335.

Kenny, M. E., Blustein, D. L., Haase, R. F., Jackson, J., & Perry, J. C. (2006). Setting the stage: Career development and the student engagement process. *Journal of Counseling Psychology, 53*, 272-279.

Lapan, R. T. (2001). Results-based comprehensive guidance and counseling programs: A framework for planning and evaluation. *Professional School Counseling, 4*(4), 289-299.

Lapan, R. T. (2004). *Career development across the K-16 years: Bridging the present to satisfying and successful futures.* Alexandria, VA: American Counseling Association.

Lapan, R. T. (2008). *More than a job: Helping your teenagers find success and satisfaction in their future careers.* Alexandria, VA: American Counseling Association.

Lapan, R. T., Aoyagi, M., & Kayson, M. (2007). Helping rural adolescents make successful post-secondary transitions: A longitudinal study. *Professional School Counseling, 10*(3), 266-272.

Lapan, R. T., Gysbers, N., Hughey, K., & Arni, T. J. (1993). Evaluating a guidance and language arts unit for high school juniors. *Journal of Counseling and Development, 71*(4), 444-451.

Lapan, R. T., Gysbers, N. C., & Kayson, M. (2007). Missouri school counselors benefit all students: *How implementing comprehensive guidance programs improves academic achievement for all Missouri students.* Jefferson City, MO: Missouri Department of Elementary and Secondary Education. Retrieved November 2, 2008, from http:// schoolweb. missouri.edu/Msca/SchoolCounselorsStudy_Jan2007.pdf.

Lapan, R. T., Gysbers, N. C., & Sun, Y. (1997). The impact of more fully implemented guidance programs on the school experiences of high school students: A statewide evaluation study. *Journal of Counseling and Development, 75*(4), 292-302.

Lee, C. C. (Ed.). (1997). *Multicultural issues in counseling: New approaches to diversity* (2nd ed.). Alexandria, VA: American Counseling Association.

Meara, N. M., & Patton, M. J. (1994). Contributions of the working alliance in the practice of career counseling. *The Career Development Quarterly, 43*, 161-177.

Mitchell, A., & Gysbers, N. C. (1978). Comprehensive school guidance and counseling programs: Planning, design, implementation, and evaluation. In *The status of guidance and counseling in schools* (pp. 23-39). Washington, DC: American Personnel and Guidance Association.

Nelson, D. E., Fox, D. G., Haslam, M., & Gardner, J. (2007). *An evaluation of Utah's comprehensive counseling and guidance program*. Salt Lake City, UT: The Institute for Behavioral Research in Creativity.

Nelson, D. E., & Gardner, J. L. (1998). *An evaluation of the comprehensive guidance program in Utah schools*. Salt Lake City, UT: Institute for Behavioral Research in Creativity.

Parsons, F. (1909). *Choosing a vocation*. Boston: Houghton-Mifflin.

Rothney, J. W. M. (1958). *Guidance practices and results*. New York: Harper.

Ryan, N. E. (1999). *Career counseling and career choice goal attainment: A meta-analytically derived model for career counseling practice*. Unpublished doctoral dissertation, Loyola University, Chicago.

Schneider, B., & Stevenson, D. (1999). *The ambitious generation: America's teenagers, motivated but directionless*. New Haven, CT: Yale University Press.

School-To-Work Opportunities Act, Pub. L. No. 103-289 (1994).

Sears, P. S., & Barbie, A. H. (1977). Career and life satisfaction among Terman's gifted women. In J. C. Stanley, W. George, & C. Solano (Eds.), *The gifted and creative: Fifty year perspective* (pp. 72-106). Baltimore: Johns Hopkins University Press.

Shadish, W. R., Cook, T. D., Campbell, D. T. (2002). *Experimental and quasi-experimental designs for generalized causal inferences.* Boston: Houghton Mifflin Company.

Sue, D. W., & Sue, D. (2008). *Counseling the culturally diverse: Theory and practice* (5th ed.). New York: Wiley.

Super, D. E., Savickas, M. L., & Super, C. M. (1996). The life-span, life-space approach to careers. In D. Brown, L. Brooks, & Associates (Eds.), *Career choice and development* (3rd ed., pp. 121-178). San Francisco: Jossey-Bass.

Wampold, B. E. (2001). *The great psychotherapy debate: Models, methods, and findings.* Mahwah, NJ: Erlbaum.

Washington State University Social and Economic Sciences Research Center. (2007). *Navigation 101: Progress to date (January, 2007).* Olympia, WA: Washington State Office of the Superintendent of Public Instruction.

Whiston, S. C., Sexton, T. L., & Lasoff, D. L. (1998). Career-intervention outcome: A replication and extension of Oliver and Spokane (1988). *Journal of Counseling Psychology, 45*(2), 150-165.

Part III:
Designing, Delivering, Evaluating,
and Advocating for Strengths-Based
Career Development in Schools

Chapter 5

Designing and Delivering Strengths-Based Career Development

The field of guidance and counseling is awash in instructional activities for all educational levels that focus on career, academic, and personal/social topics. Nor are there shortages of materials and resources on these topics. And yet, even with all of the instructional activities, materials, and resources available, professional school counselors continue to struggle with how best to design and deliver guidance and counseling activities in general and career guidance and counseling activities designed around strengths-based career development concepts specifically.

Chapter 5 responds to these struggles by describing how professional school counselors, working closely with parents, teachers, and administrators, can design and deliver strengths-based career development within the framework of comprehensive guidance and counseling programs. The chapter first focuses on guidelines for designing career guidance and counseling activities. Then, full discussion is provided on how career guidance and counseling activities can be delivered to all students in grades K-12 through the comprehensive guidance and counseling program components of guidance curriculum, individual student planning, responsive services, and systems support.

Designing Career Guidance and Counseling Activities

Design: To plan and fashion skillfully
(*Random House Webster's Unabridged Dictionary*, 2001, p. 539)

Planning and fashioning career guidance and counseling activities skillfully requires attention to a number of key issues. These issues include the design process to be used, effective learning strategies identification and use, assumptions about learning, and an appropriate format for career guidance and counseling activities. This section of Chapter 5 discusses these issues in detail.

The Backward Design Process

The design of career guidance and counseling activities is guided by national, state, and local standards that specify the knowledge, skills, and attitudes students need to acquire. These standards, when infused with strengths-based career development content, are the outcomes that students are expected to acquire as a result of their participation in the career guidance and counseling activities of comprehensive guidance and counseling programs. They are the learning outcomes of career guidance and counseling activities.

To "plan and fashion skillfully" career guidance and counseling activities, the use of a curricular design process called "backward design" is recommended (Wiggins & McTighe, 1998). Career guidance and counseling activities are the means. Standards representing outcomes are the ends. In the backward design process, standards (outcomes) are stated first, and then activities are designed to assist students to acquire the learning outcomes expressed as standards.

In the backward design process, evaluation is first, not last. According to Wiggins and McTighe (1998), it is important to first decide on the evidence that is acceptable that indicates students have acquired the knowledge, skills, and attitudes specified in the standards before designing any activities. Individuals who have used this process reported that "thinking like an assessor about evidence or learning not only helps them to clarify their goals but also results in a more sharply defined teaching and learning target, so that students perform better knowing their goals" (Wiggins & McTighe, p. 9).

The backwards design process consists of the following steps (SuccessLink, n.d.):

1. Identify the desired outcomes (standards).
   • What should students know?
   • What should students be able to do?
2. Determine the acceptable evidence of achievement.
   • What kind of evidence is required?
   • What specific characteristics in student responses, products, or performances should be examined?
   • Can levels of students' knowledge, skills, and attitudes be inferred from the proposed evidence?
3. Plan learning activities based on desired outcomes (standards).

A Learning Theory Perspective

Before career guidance and counseling activities are designed and written it is important to note some basic assumptions about the nature of learning. Listed below are five important assumptions about human learning that need to be considered in the design and writing phase because they affect the nature and structure of the activities to be written and used with students. The five assumptions are:

1. Individual development is a process of continuous and sequential (but not necessarily uninterrupted or uniform) progress toward increased effectiveness in the management and mastery of the environment for the satisfaction of psychological and social needs.
2. The stage, or level, or individuals' development at any given point is related to the nature and accuracy of their perceptions, the level of complexity of their conceptualizations, and the subsequent development rate and direction. No individual in an educational setting is at a zero point in development; hence change must be measured from some relative point rather than from an absolute.
3. Positive developmental changes are potential steps toward the achievement of higher level purposive goals. This interlocking relationship dictates that achievement at a particular growth stage be viewed as a means to further development rather than as an end result.
4. Environmental or situational variables provide the external dimension of individual development. Knowledge, understanding, skills, attitudes, values, and aspirations are the product of the interaction of these external variables with the internal variables that characterize the individual.
5. The developmental learning process moves from a beginning level of awareness and differentiation (perceptualization), to the next level of conceptualizing relationships and meanings (conceptualization), to the highest level of behavioral consistency and effectiveness by both internal and external evaluation (generalization). (Wellman & Moore, 1975, pp. 55-56)

How do these five assumptions about learning effect the development, layout, and use of career guidance and counseling activities in grades K-12? Think of them as explanations about how learning unfolds, explanations that need to be understood and incorporated into the design and implementation of career guidance and counseling activities. The first assumption underscores the point that career guidance and counseling content and activities need to be provided systematically over time to students, preferably from K through grade 12. Assumption two points out that how individuals perceive and conceptualize knowledge plays a role in their acquisition of that knowledge. It also suggests that individuals are not empty vessels; they have ideas about the knowledge they are to learn (Larson & Keiper, 2007). Assumption three highlights the fact that achievement occurs developmentally; it is a means, not an end, while assumption four underscores the important interplay of external and internal factors in the learning process. Finally, assumption five stresses that learning progresses from perceptualizations, to conceptualizations, to generalizations.

In designing career guidance and counseling activities, pay attention to the three phases of learning, perceptualization, conceptualization, and generalization. The activities need to be designed so that students can become aware of the career or related knowledge, skills, and attitudes to be learned, can differentiate the material, make connections to previous learning, internalize the material, and then generalize or apply and reflect on the material.

Another way to consider designing career guidance and counseling activities is to use the cognitive process model (Anderson et al., 2001). The process model is a revision of a taxonomy developed by Bloom, Engelhart, Furst, Hill, and Krathwohl (1956). The cognitive process model contains six phases including remember, understand, apply, analyze, evaluate, and create. Each of these is defined as follows:

1. REMEMBER—Retrieve relevant knowledge from long-term memory
2. UNDERSTAND—Construct meaning from instructional messages, including oral, written, and graphic communication.
3. APPLY—Carry out or use a procedure in a given situation.
4. ANALYZE—Break material into its constituent parts and determine how the parts relate to one another and to an overall structure or purpose.
5. EVALUATE—Make judgments based on criteria and standards
6. CREATE—Put elements together to form a coherent or functional whole; reorganize elements into a new pattern or structure. (Anderson et al. 2001, p. 31)

A Sample Format

An important consideration in designing career guidance and counseling activities is deciding on the format to use. This is an important decision because the format that is chosen dictates how activities are arranged. This decision also dictates the kind and amount of information to be included as well.

There are many different ways to format career guidance and counseling activities. We recommend that the format used should be the same format that is used in the school district by other educational disciplines such as mathematics, science, and language arts. What does such a format look like? To illustrate we present a format created by SuccessLink, an organization funded by the Missouri Department of Elementary and Secondary

Education to develop and disseminate the best teaching ideas for all disciplines throughout Missouri. By using this format, guidance and counseling, including career guidance and counseling, is identified as a regular and integral program within the educational system of Missouri.

In Appendix A is an example career guidance and counseling unit titled "How Do the Pieces Fit?" designed for use with 7th graders. It uses the Success Link format and was developed by Missouri professional school counselors and counselor educators as part of the state of Missouri's development of example lessons for the Guidance Curriculum of the Missouri Comprehensive Guidance Program. To see all of the example units in the career domain, as well as those in the academic and personal-social domains, visit the following website: mcce.org.

Notice that the example uses the curriculum unit as the organizer for the lessons. Why use the curriculum units as organizers for lessons? According to Anderson et al. (2001), units are recommended because they provide the time for more complete and integrated learning, more flexibility in time use, the background and context for understanding specific lesson objectives, and more time to allow for student learning and the assessment of such learning.

Notice too that in this example there is a unit overview followed by the details of each lesson. In the overview, the overall unit content is crosswalked to the American School Counselor Association National Standards, the State of Missouri Show Me Standards, Academic Content Areas, and Enduring Life Skills. This procedure anchors the career guidance unit to the academic programs of the state and district as well as the American School Counselor Association. The overview, as well as the three lessons that follow, also uses the term grade level expectation (GLE) to focus on the specific knowledge, skills, and attitudes students will acquire in each lesson. The use of the phrase grade level expectations (GLE) is important because in Missouri, all teachers use the same phrase to specify the content they are teaching. Thus the district's comprehensive guidance and counseling program and its curriculum component uses the same language that all teachers use.

Delivering Career Guidance and Counseling Activities

The three major direct delivery program components for career guidance and counseling for all students are the guidance curriculum, individual student planning, and responsive services components of comprehensive guidance and counseling programs. The guidance curriculum consists of career content as well as academic and personal/social content organized as guidance and counseling activities specified by grade levels and presented systematically in grades K-12. The guidance curriculum "is a specific plan with identified lessons in an appropriate form and sequence for directing teaching" (Wiggins & McTighe, 1998, p. 4). Individual student planning, on the other hand, focuses on assuring that all students beginning in middle school develop and use personal plans of study as they progress through the school years and beyond into postsecondary education or work. The activities of the guidance curriculum provide students with needed knowledge, skills, and attitudes while the individual student planning component assists students to use the knowledge, skills, and attitudes acquired from their experiences in the guidance curriculum to develop and use personal plans of study to guide their work in school and to make successful transitions to work or postsecondary education. Responsive services provides students with the opportunity to meet one to one with school counselors to discuss career, academic, and personal/social concerns or to participate in small groups of students dealing with career, academic, or personal/social issues.

Seven Effective Learning Strategies

Before discussion proceeds concerning the three major delivery program components for career guidance and counseling for all students, it is important to review learning strategies that can facilitate student acquisition of important career guidance and counseling knowledge, skills, and attitudes (guidance curriculum) that form the foundation for successful career planning, goal setting, and decision making (individual student planning and responsive services). For our purpose, we define learning strategies as "any activities, techniques, or procedures used by learners to enhance their understanding of or to improve their performance or learning tasks" (Lapan, Kardash, & Turner, 2002, p. 263). Research has identified seven types of effective learning strategies that can facilitate student success that merit attention. They need to be incorporated into and guide the application of career guidance and counseling activities when and where possible as these activities are delivered to all students through the guidance curriculum, individual student planning, and responsive services. They are presented in Table 5-1.

Assisting Students to Use Effective Learning Strategies

Ormrod (1999) contended that the reason students do not use effective learning strategies is that they have not been taught them nor have they been taught when, where, and how to use them. The best way for professional school counselors to assist students to use effective learning strategies is in the context of actual career guidance and counseling activities; on real learning

Table 5-1

Seven Types of Effective Learning Strategies

1. Identification of important information. The ability to separate important from nonessential information by paying attention to "signaling devices" – underlined and highlighted words and phrases as well as story grammars that structure information (Mandler, 1984; Ormrod, 1999).

2. Summarizing. The identification of main ideas and the creation of super ordinate concepts that subsume and integrate more specific information (Ormrod, 1999).

3. Activation of prior knowledge. Relating new information to information the student already knows. When students draw inferences or generate new examples, they can more effectively add to, expand upon, and elaborate new information by making connections to previously learned material (Gagne, Yekovich, & Yekovich, 1993).

4. Notetaking. Effective notetaking requires the student to summarize main ideas and include details that support those concepts (Ormrod, 1999).

5. Organization. The process of dividing the information to be learned into subsets and indicating the relationships among subsets (Gagne et al., 1993). Examples include: determining which words in a list to be remembered are related in some way and grouping them together; creating an outline of major topics and ideas; creating graphic representations of the material to be remembered; and developing concept maps.

6. Comprehension monitoring. Having students stop and periodically ask themselves whether they are truly understanding what they are reading or learning and taking steps to remediate any comprehension difficulties they are experiencing (Baker, 1989). Self-questioning techniques can be particularly effective by having students formulate questions before, throughout, and after a lesson or a reading assignment. Such strategies can be used in peer tutoring formats.

7. Imagery. Teaching students to construct internal images that represent the meaning of the text that is being read or studied. Mnemonic imagery is especially helpful for learning lists, pairs of words, and isolated facts (Ormrod, 1999).

Note: From "Empowering Students to become Self-Regulated Learners," by R. T. Lapan, C. M. Kardash, and S. Turner, 2002, *Professional School Counseling, 5*, p. 263. Copyright 2002 by the American School Counselor Association. Used with permission.

Table 5-2

Assisting Students to Use Effective Learning Strategies

---

1. Explain the strategy to students, tell them the types of tasks for which it is helpful, and explain to them why it is helpful (Ormrod, 1999). Such knowledge makes it more likely that students will generalize the strategy to other, similar learning tasks.
2. Model the strategy for students, thinking aloud as you do so (Brown & Palincsar, as cited in Ormrod, 1999). As students learn how to execute the strategies independently, you can gradually fade out your supportive structuring of their attempts.
3. Have students practice effective strategies on a variety of learning tasks, across the curriculum, and on an ongoing basis (Brown & Palincsar, as cited in Ormrod, 1999). This will help to promote both generalization and maintenance of the strategy.
4. Show students the concrete benefits of strategy use by having them evaluate their performance on learning tasks both with and without applying the strategies (Harris & Pressley, 1991).
5. Have students rehearse the use of both overt and covert strategies (Kardash & Amlund, 1991). Overt strategies are those that can be seen (e.g., underlining, note taking). Covert strategies are internal mental processes (e.g., imagery, relating new information to prior knowledge).
6. Have students practice learning strategies with their peers (Ormrod, 1999).
7. Help students to develop ways to monitor and evaluate their own performance, and actively involve students in the modification and construction of new strategies (Harris & Pressley, 1991).

Note: From "Empowering Students to Become Self-Regulated Learners," by R. T. Lapan, C. M. Kardash, and S. Turner, 2002, *Professional School Counseling, 5*, p. 264. Copyright 2002 by the American School Counselor Association. Used with permission.

tasks and assignments, giving students plenty of opportunities to learn and practice their new learning strategies.

Table 5-2 presents seven guidelines school counselors can incorporate in their career guidance and counseling activities and the processes they use to teach them to fully engage students in learning. The goal is to connect students to what is to be learned so that they can become self-regulated learners.

The Goal: Self Regulated Learners

The goal of comprehensive guidance and counseling programs featuring strength-based career development content delivered through career guidance and counseling activities is to create self-regulated learners.

What is self-regulated learning? In Figure 5-1, Lapan, Kardash, and Turner (2002) pointed out that for optimal self-regulated learning to take place, schools, families, and communities must all play a part. They identified three steps that are involved in self-regulated learning. Step 1 describes key behaviors that students exhibit as self-regulated learning unfolds. Step 2 points out the importance of extrinsic and intrinsic motivation. Step 3 stresses that full engagement in learning results in positive outcomes.

When students are self-regulated learners, they are more likely to feel connected to school. In an article titled "Wingspread Declaration on School Connections" (2004), the importance of students feeling connected to school was highlighted. "Increasing the number of students connected to school is likely to impact critical accountability measures, such as: academic performance, incidents of fighting, bullying, or vandalism, absenteeism, and school completion rates" (p. 233).

Figure 5-1

School, Family, and Community Contexts that Promote Self-Regulated Learning

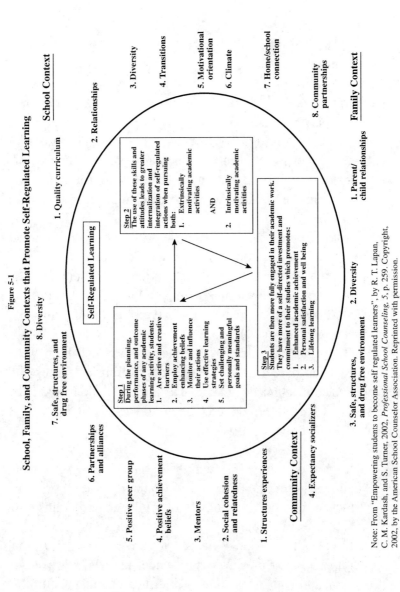

Note: From "Empowering students to become self regulated learners", by R. T. Lapan,
C. M. Kardash, and S. Turner, 2002, *Professional School Counseling*, 5, p. 259. Copyright,
2002, by the American School Counselor Association. Reprinted with permission.

The Delivery System

Guidance Curriculum

Guidance curriculum activities are delivered to all students through:

- Classroom activities: School counselors teach, team teach, or support the teaching of guidance curriculum activities or units in classrooms. Teachers also may teach such units. The guidance curriculum is not limited to being taught in one or two subjects but should include as many subjects as possible in the total school curriculum. These activities may be conducted in the classroom, guidance center, or other school facilities.
- Schoolwide activities: School counselors organize and conduct large group sessions such as career days and educational/college/career days. Other members of the guidance and counseling team, including teachers and administrators, also may be involved in organizing and conducting such sessions.

Given the vehicles of the classroom and school wide activities, what career guidance and counseling activities and related academic and personal/social activities should be included in a school district's guidance curriculum? Several sources of information help answer this question.

1. Review carefully the strengths-based career development content found in Table 3-1 in Chapter 3 and incorporate these outcomes into all career guidance and counseling activities in grades K-12.
2. Review the mission of the district and the district's school improvement plan for cues concerning the knowledge, skills, and attitudes (standards) students must acquire.

3. Conduct a needs assessment using the guidance content standards of the district to obtain information about which standards students, parents, and teachers value.
4. Establish the amount of time at the elementary, middle, and high school levels deemed necessary to devote to career guidance and counseling activities as well as the related academic and personal/social activities.
5. Lay out a school year calendar by each month specifying what, when, and where career guidance and counseling activities as well as the related academic and personal/social activities will be conducted considering the use of the classroom as well as the overall school wide activities.

What would the layout of a guidance curriculum featuring career guidance and counseling look like that followed these recommendations? The layout would look similar to the guidance curriculum in the Granite School District in Utah. The guidance curriculum in the Granite District has three domains, self discovery, life skills, and future planning. The curriculum is designed to address school goals and needs (Granite School District Comprehensive Counseling and Guidance Program, 2006).

How is the guidance curriculum delivered in the Granite District in grades 7-12? Classroom guidance curriculum activities are delivered to all students, all grades, at least once each grading term. Some counselors collaborate with English teachers to take 20 minutes of classroom instruction time for guidance curriculum "quick stops". Others organize "break outs" through social studies classes where they deliver guidance curriculum to students in their individual caseloads, by class period (p. 2).

How do Granite School district school counselors lay out the guidance curriculum? Table 5-3 presents a sample layout of topics for grades 7-12 focusing on the four terms of Granite's school year. At the top of the table note that the word orientation is used for the first term followed by the three content domains for the next three school year terms. Then on the left side are grades 7-12 with a theme for each year. Then the topics to be covered are presented by school terms. Lesson plans are written for each topic that describe what is to be learned, the activities involved, and ways the lessons are evaluated.

Once the topics have been arranged by grade and school year term, the next step is to work with teachers to arrange times for classroom guidance curriculum activities. Table 5-4 presents an example focusing on 10th grade English with 13 sections. Note how the Granite school counselors worked with the English teachers to schedule their lessons.

Individual Student Planning: An Overview

Our children must learn to understand and plan their life with a view beyond graduation. Keys to the success of this effort are the empowerment of young people to take control of their future; the strong relationship built between student, teacher/counselor and involved parents; and the accountability and responsibility that the students take on to meet their goals. No student is overlooked or lost; each has the opportunity to plan for and work towards a future that he or she believes in. These skills are essential preparation for the workplace that they will be entering. (Miller, as cited in Severn, 2004, p. 24)

The foundation for student planning is established during the elementary school years through guidance curriculum activities. Self-concept development, the acquisition of learning-to-learning skills, interpersonal relationship skill development,

Table 5-3

Guidance Curriculum Layout Example: Granite School

	Orientation 1st Term What do students need to know to navigate the school system?	**Self Discovery** 2nd Term What do students need to know about self concept, respect for self and others, etc.?	**Life Skills** 3rd Term What do students need to know about making decisions, connecting school to work, life-long learning, etc.?	**Future Planning** 4th Term What do students need to know about planning for their next steps?
7th Grade **Explore**	"Learn the Language of Junior High" (7.0)	"Defense Against the Dark Acts" (7.1c)	TLC CDA Activity #10 "Recognizing Values" (7.2b)	TLC CDA Activity #6 "Personality and Career" (7.3b)
8th Grade **Expand**	"Secrets to School Success" (8.0)	"Choose Your Attitude" (8.1a)	"Work, a Positive Experience" (8.1c)	"Choices Today Lead to Opportunities Tomorrow" (8.3a)
9th Grade **Plan**	"The First Official Year of High School" (9.0)	"Accept Responsibility for Your Choices" (9.1a)	"Set Goals, Me?" (9.2b)	"Preparing for Life After High School" (9.3a)

continued on page 146

Table 5-3 (continued)

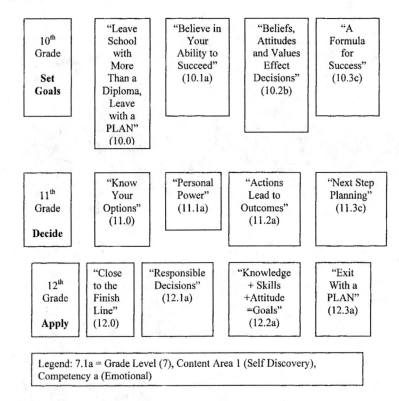

10th Grade **Set Goals**	"Leave School with More Than a Diploma, Leave with a PLAN" (10.0)	"Believe in Your Ability to Succeed" (10.1a)	"Beliefs, Attitudes and Values Effect Decisions" (10.2b)	"A Formula for Success" (10.3c)
11th Grade **Decide**	"Know Your Options" (11.0)	"Personal Power" (11.1a)	"Actions Lead to Outcomes" (11.2a)	"Next Step Planning" (11.3c)
12th Grade **Apply**	"Close to the Finish Line" (12.0)	"Responsible Decisions" (12.1a)	"Knowledge + Skills +Attitude =Goals" (12.2a)	"Exit With a PLAN" (12.3a)

Legend: 7.1a = Grade Level (7), Content Area 1 (Self Discovery), Competency a (Emotional)

Note: From *Granite School District Comprehensive Counseling and Guidance Program Scope and Sequence Guidance Curriculum Activities,* 2006, Salt Lake City, UT: Granite School District. Used with permission.

Table 5-4

Scheduling Classroom Lessons

	Orientation	Self Discovery	Life Skills	Future Planning
	1st Term	2nd Term	3rd Term	4th Term
10th Grade	"Leave school with more than a diploma!" (10.0)			

Subject Area – 10th Grade English (13 Sections)

10th Grade English	Monday	Tuesday	Wednesday	Thursday	Friday
1st/5th	Campbell 105 (Counselor A)	Wheeler 221 (Counselor C)			
	Smith 204 (Counselor B)	Johnson 222 (Counselor B)			
2nd/6th	Campbell 105 (Counselor C)	Campbell 105 (Counselor A)			
	Smith 204 (Counselor A)	Johnson 222 (Counselor C)			
3rd/7th	Johnson 222 (Counselor B)	Johnson 222 (Counselor A)			
	Campbell 105 (Counselor C)				
4th/8th	Smith 204 (Counselor A)	Wheeler 221 (Counselor B)			

Note: From *Granite School District Comprehensive Counseling and Guidance Program Scope and Sequence Guidance Curriculum Activities*, 2006, Salt Lake City, UT: Granite School District. Used with permission.

decision-making skill building, and awareness and beginning exploration of educational and occupational possibilities are sample subjects that are covered during these years. Subjects such as these continue to be covered through the guidance curriculum component during middle school and high school, providing new information and experiences to enable students to regularly update, monitor, and manage their plans effectively.

Building on the foundation provided in elementary school, beginning planning for the future is undertaken during the middle school years through the individual student planning component. During this period, students' plans focus on high school course selection, taking into account graduation requirements and the requirements of their postsecondary educational and occupational goals. Guidance curriculum activities continue to support and guide the planning process.

During the high school years, plans developed in the middle school are reviewed and updated periodically in accordance with students' postsecondary personal, educational, and career goals. The individual student planning component provides time for regular individual work with students as well as group sessions focusing on individual student planning. Guidance curriculum activities continue to support student planning by giving emphasis to the development and use of decision-making, goal-setting, and planning skills. The importance and relevance of basic academic and career and technical skills are stressed. The goal is for students' plans to become pathways or guides through which students can use the past and present to anticipate and prepare for the future.

Individual student planning is implemented through such strategies as:

- Individual appraisal: School counselors assist students to assess and interpret their abilities, interests, skills, and achievement.

- Individual advisement: School counselors assist students to use self-appraisal information along with personal/social, academic, career, and labor market information to help them plan for and realize their personal, social, academic, and career goals.
- Transition planning: School counselors and other education personnel assist students to make the transition from school to work or to additional education and training.

Student plans that are developed as a result of individual student planning activities come in a variety of formats. One format is the traditional 4-year high school plan. It focuses on high school course selection consistent with meeting high school graduation and postsecondary education goal requirements. Another format that is being used increasingly is the student portfolio either in a paper or electronic form (Davis, 1997). The portfolio is much more comprehensive than a 4-year plan. It is designed to help students record and document their work, their education and training, as well as the personal experiences they have had and the skills they have acquired. It may have a job performance part with sections presenting personal, educational, and work-record information and primary job skills. Another part often presents work interests, traits, and attitudes; special training or skills; favorite classes, training programs, subjects, and educational activities; and social/leisure activities. Still another format is the career passport. It contains some of the same information found in the portfolio but is less detailed and concentrates more on information needed for job interviews and job applications.

When students leave school, they take their life career plan folders with them. Whether they go to work or continue their education, the folder and the accompanying competency lists are available for additional goal-setting, decision-making, and planning activities. Information in the folder can assist them in a variety of job-seeking and job-keeping activities, including filling out application forms, writing resumes, developing curriculum vitae, or preparing for job advancement. As new experiences are acquired, they can be analyzed and added to the appropriate sections of the folder. Thus the individual life career plan folder with accompanying competency lists can become an ongoing goal-setting and planning vehicle for individuals as long as they with to use it.

Educational and career decision making, planning, and goal setting are primarily the responsibility of students and their parents or guardians. Parent and guardian involvement in the activities of the individual student planning component is essential to students' successful development and implementation of education and career plans. For student planning to be effective, parents or guardians need accurate information in a timely manner as guidance and counseling activities are implemented.

The life career plans that students develop and use are both processes and instruments. As processes, students' plans evolve throughout the school years responding to successions of the learning activities in the overall school program as well as the guidance activities provided through the guidance curriculum and individual planning components of the guidance program. As instruments, plans provide structured ways for students to gather, analyse, synthesize, and organize self, educational, and occupational information. As processes, plans are vehicles through which this information is incorporated into short- and long-range goal setting, decision-making, and planning activities. As instruments, plans are not tracks to be plotted and followed routinely; they are, instead, blueprints for life quests (Gysbers, 1985).

Individual Student Planning in Action

What does individual planning with students look like in action? Two examples are provided. The first example is from the Granite School District in Utah. The Granite district has implemented the Utah State requirement that every student in grades 7-12 have a Student Education and Occupation Plan (SEOP). The second example is from the Franklin Pierce School District in Washington. The Franklin Pierce District developed an individual student planning system that has evolved into a statewide system titled "Navigation 101" (Severn, 2004).

Granite School District.

In the Granite District, the SEOP is the form and the process through which individual student planning unfolds. The goal is to assist students in grades 7-12 to plan, monitor, and manage their own learning as well as their personal and career development. Students can set, review, and evaluate their educational, personal, and career goals connecting them to activities that help them achieve their goals. The SEOP process is career guidance and counseling in action.

School counselors in the Granite School District have set a goal they call the 3x4 plan. The 3x4 plan means that in every middle and high school, school counselors or other educational personnel will have three individual SEOP planning meetings with each student (every school year), and at least one meeting with a parent or guardian in attendance. They will also conduct four classroom guidance activities, one activity each term for each grade level, grades 7-12 (Granite School District Comprehensive Counseling and Guidance Program, 2006).

The key to putting the 3x4 plan into full operation is calendaring. Calendaring individual student planning in the Granite District began with the decision of what percentage of time school counselors should devote to the planning process at the middle school and high school. Then, that percentage of school counselor time was translated into days of the school year and into the class periods available. Next the ratio of school counselors to students was added to determine how much time each school counselor could spend with each student and in preparing for individual sessions. In the 2005-2006 school year, 95% of the students met at least once with their school counselor while 52% of the parents involved met at least once with their students and a school counselor (Granite School District Comprehensive Counseling and Guidance Program, 2006, p. 2).

Franklin Pierce School District.

According to Severn (2004) the foundation of individual student planning is the guidance curriculum. Navigation 101, the title of the individual planning part of the curriculum, uses an advisor-advisee system in which teachers and school counselors meet twice a month with groups of 20 students. The Navigation 101 coursework includes:

- discussion and analysis of students' test results,
- various assessments of personal interests and aptitudes,
- goal-setting skill development,
- planning for each year's high school course selection and personal goals,
- independent living skills lessons, such as how to budget and how to balance a checkbook,
- information about how the postsecondary education and training system works and how to access it, and
- development of a student portfolio and planning for annual, student-led planning conferences with their parents or guardians and the Navigation teacher (Severn, 2004, p. 10).

The individual student planning part of Navigation 101 begins in 6th grade when students develop a portfolio. In the spring, conferences are held with students and parents or guardians to review student plans and progress. The interesting feature of these conferences is that students plan and lead them. They discuss what they have done and then describe their future plans. When the conferences end all individuals involved sign the students' plans (Severn, 2004).

What are the results of this system? According to the Franklin Pierce School District website, evaluation studies indicated:

- A 10% increase in the number of students who progress from 9th to 10th grade on time.
- An 8% decline in students receiving an F in one or more classes.
- Dramatic increases in the number of students enrolling in rigorous, demanding classes: 28% increase in students requesting pre-calculus classes; 240% increase in students requesting physics classes, and 180% increase in students requesting chemistry classes.
- A school-wide transition to a more student-centered, individualized way of thinking about education.

In addition, the system revealed a new way of creating school schedules in which students register first, and then school officials plan the class schedule to respond to students' preferences.

Responsive Services

Some students need career guidance and counseling assistance beyond what is provided in the guidance curriculum or in individual student planning activities. They need the opportunity to discuss their educational and career plans directly with a professional, a school counselor. They may find that the counseling relationship in individual counseling allows them to talk openly and freely about who they are, their present circumstances, and their future career plans that they could not do in guidance curriculum and individual student planning activities. They can talk about these issues privately and in confidence.

Individual counseling can provide in depth time to use a variety of career counseling techniques not available in other intervention modalities. For example, qualitative career assessments such as card sorts, structured interviews, and geneograms fit nicely in individual counseling sessions (Gysbers, Heppner, & Johnston, 2009). These assessments are based on constructivism theory, a type of learning theory that describes how individuals construct their own ideas about their worlds as they try to make sense out of their experiences. They provide a means for individuals to reflect on their real-life experiences through the use of narratives, enabling them to construct understandings of their situations and circumstances.

Individual counseling can also provide opportunities to use educational and career information to assist students as they consider their options. Such information can be tailored to students' needs as individual counseling sessions unfold. Time can be devoted to fully processing information that is difficult to do in other interventions.

Small-group, short-term career issue groups also may be useful to some students as they consider their next steps educationally and occupationally. Such groups may provide opportunities for discussions that can expand and extend students' perceptions about themselves and the possibilities that are available to them that go beyond what they might experience in guidance curriculum career guidance and counseling activities.

Kraus (2006) stated that small group career issue groups are powerful mediums. He suggested that such groups engage students in active learning, help them with their interpersonal communication, and help them open up to others. He identified the following types of groups that might be formed at elementary, middle, and high school levels:

> Career-play groups in early elementary programs, or 'explore your interests' groups; career-shadowing groups in middle schools and academic and career-direction groups in middle and high schools; college application essay groups, job interview groups, considering military service groups. (p. 2)

Summing Up

"When high school seniors have more fully integrated critical career development skills into their school lives and how they are approaching impending postsecondary transitions, they are more likely to have measurable advantages in young adulthood" (Lapan, Aoyagi, & Kayson, 2007).

The evidence is clear. Students who have experienced career guidance and counseling activities infused with strengths-based career development content, organized and carried out within a comprehensive guidance and counseling program framework, do better in school and in their transitions educationally and occupationally. As a result, school counselors must make sure that these activities "are consistently and competently provided to all students" (Lapan, Aoyagi, & Kayson, 2007).

References

Anderson, L. W., Krathwohl, D. R., Airasian, P. W., Cruikshank, K. A., Mayer, R. E., Pintrich, P. R., et al. (Eds.). (2001). *A taxonomy for learning, teaching, and assessing*. New York: Addison Wesley Longman, Inc.

Baker, L. (1989). Metacognition, comprehension monitoring, and the adult reader. *Educational Psychology Review, 1*, 3-38.

Bloom, B. S., Engelhart, M. D., Furst, E. J., Hill, W. H., & Krathwohl, D. R. (1956). *Taxonomy of educational objectives: Handbook I: Cognitive domain*. New York: David McKay.

Davis, D. (1997). The comprehensive guidance program in Davis County schools. In N. C. Gysbers & P. Henderson (Eds.), *Comprehensive guidance programs that work—II* (pp. 107-123). Greensboro, NC: ERIC Counseling and Student Services Clearinghouse.

Gagne, E. D., Yekovich, C. W., & Yekovich, F. R. (1993). *The cognitive psychology of school learning*. New York: Harper Collins.

Granite School District Comprehensive Counseling and Guidance Program. (2006). *School counselor update*. Salt Lake City, UT: Author.

Gysbers, N. C. (1985). *Create and use an individual career development plan*. Wooster, OH: Bell & Howell Publications System Division.

Gysbers, N. C., Heppner, M. J., & Johnston, J. A. (2009). *Career counseling: Process, issues, and techniques* (3rd Ed.). Alexandria, VA: American Counseling Association.

Harris, K. R., & Pressley, M. (1991). The nature of cognitive strategy instruction: Interactive strategy instruction. *Exceptional Children, 57*, 392-404.

Kardash, C. A. M., & Amlund, J. (1991). Self-reported learning strategies and learning from expository text. *Contemporary Educational Psychology 16*, 117-138.

Kraus, K. L. (2006, June). Leading career development (psychoeducational) groups in schools. *Career Convergence*. Retrieved July 3, 2006, from 209. 235.208.145/cgi-bin/AWS.pl?NCDA,130285,DTP,AWS_NCDA2_careerconvergence.html.

Lapan, R. T., Aoyagi, M., & Kayson, M. (2007). Helping rural adolescents make successful postsecondary transitions: A longitudinal study. *Professional School Counseling, 10*, 266-272.

Lapan, R. T., Kardash, C. M., & Turner, S. (2002). Empowering students to become self-regulated learners. *Professional School Counseling, 5*, 257-265.

Larson, B. E., & Keiper, T. A. (2007). *Instructional strategies for middle and high school*. New York: Routledge.

Mandler, J. M. (1984). *Stories, scripts, and scenes: Aspects of schema theory*. Hillsdale, NJ: Lawrence Erlbaum.

Ormrod, J. E. (1999). *Human learning* (3rd ed.). Upper Saddle River, NJ: Merrill.

Random House Webster's Unabridged Dictionary (2nd ed.). (2001). New York: Random House.

Severn, J. (2004). *Navigation 101: How to focus on planning skills leads to higher student performance*. Olympia, WA: Office of Superintendent of Public Instruction.

SuccessLink (n.d.). *SuccessLink backward lesson design in-service*. Jefferson City, MO: Author. (www.successlink.org)

Washington State University Social and Economic Sciences Research Center. (2007). Navigation 101: Progress to date (January, 2007). Olympia, WA: Washington State Office of the Superintendent of Public Instruction. Retrieved from www.k12.wa.us

Wellman, F. E., & Moore, E. J. (1975). *Pupil personnel services: A handbook for program development and evaluation.* Washington, DC: U.S. Department of Health, Education, and Welfare.

Wiggins, G., & McTighe, J. (1998). *Understanding by design.* Alexandria, VA: Association for Supervision and Curriculum Development.

Wingspread declaration on school connections. (2004). *Journal of School Health, 74,* 233-234.

Chapter 6

Evaluating Career Guidance and Counseling Activities

This chapter presents strategies and activities professional school counselors and other educational professionals can use to evaluate strengths-based career guidance and counseling activities. First, a rationale for why evaluation is necessary is provided. Then, a practical action research approach for conducting results-based evaluation is described. Next, a method for doing an evaluation audit of the career guidance and counseling activities currently in use in a school building or district is outlined. And finally, readers can complete a reflective practice exercise to assess the level of implementation of strengths-based career guidance and counseling activities in their schools.

Part One:
Why Evaluate Career Guidance and Counseling Activities?

We evaluate career guidance and counseling activities in a comprehensive program because this is one of the best ways to enhance and improve the services provided to all students in our schools. Gysbers and Henderson (2006) described the five phases of comprehensive program development (i.e., planning, design, implementation, evaluation, and enhancement). Program planning sets the stage for the design of specific activities and interventions in a school. Once designed, the program can be implemented. Only after a program is implemented can it be evaluated. Given the results of the evaluation, counselors can use this information to enhance and improve their program. As Slavin (2002) so nicely stated, "program evaluation is a dynamic that motivates a pace of innovation and improvement." In comprehensive guidance and counseling programs, evaluation empowers key stakeholders (e.g., professional school counselors, administrators, students, and parents) to sustain a process that leads inevitably to creating innovative ways to better help all students.

A second reason professional school counselors engage in program evaluation activities is that it increases their ability to be reflective, investigative professionals. Borrowing from Ruth Garner's work (1990), evaluating program activities helps to enhance the fund of descriptive, procedural, and metacognitive knowledge necessary for the skilled performance of any complex job task. For example, by engaging in program evaluation activities that are both practical and rigorous we learn more about those outcomes that should be realized by career guidance and counseling interventions. This adds to the declarative knowledge we have about how to do our job. Second, by evaluating our programs we better learn how to bring about the results that we want. This increases the procedural knowledge available to us. And finally, by seriously undertaking program evaluation efforts we become more aware of the situations in which different career guidance and counseling interventions are successful and why they are successful. This broadens our metacognitive knowledge that is absolutely essential for expert performance of the complex work tasks that face all educational professionals. Enhanced declarative, procedural, and metacognitive knowledge brings us closer to the ideal of knowing what career guidance and counseling interventions work for which students under what conditions (Herr & Cramer, 1972).

A third reason professional school counselors should engage in program evaluation efforts is the advocacy mission of a comprehensive guidance and counseling program. Demonstrating that a more fully implemented program leads to enhanced student success will also increase the public's acceptance, trust, and support for professional school counselors. Developing interventions that are clearly associated with better outcomes for all students will help us to successfully advocate with policymakers for the resources and support necessary to run quality comprehensive programs. Without doubt, program evaluation is an opportunity that professional school counselors should eagerly embrace.

Comprehensive guidance and counseling programs are not data driven. Our programs are student driven. We use data to improve our interventions and learn how to better serve all students in our schools. From this solid foundation, professional school counselors can then advocate with policymakers for the resources necessary to operate evidence-based comprehensive programs.

Part Two: IDEAS!

IDEAS! is an action research strategy professional school counselors and other educational professionals can use to conduct results-based program evaluation (Lapan, 2005). Professional school counselors first identify (**I**) a critical problem that needs to be investigated. Then, a reflective professional describes (**D**) the problem and the context thoroughly. After doing this, existing (**E**) school data is used to provide information relevant to answering the questions posed by this problem. Existing school data are then analyzed (**A**) by professional school counselors using 5 basic statistical procedures, qualitative data analysis skills, and easy to use software that is freely available on the

Internet. After analyzing the data, the findings are summarized (*S*) in user-friendly ways. And finally, we must not be content to share the results with only a few people. We must use the data (**!**) to help our students and advocate for the resources we need to run effective comprehensive guidance and counseling programs. This means that we need to inform key stakeholders (e.g., school administrators, parents, community leaders, and school board members) about what we are doing and how we are helping students. A more complete description of each step in the IDEAS! process is presented below.

I (Identify a critical problem)

An effective evaluation process begins by identifying the critical issues and problems that adversely affect student success. Or, conversely, we need to articulate the things that are really helping all students to succeed and figure out how to provide them with more of what we know works. Our goal is to not only promote student success, it is also to unleash the inherent motivation in students to excel in their accomplishments and relationships with others. To get started, professional school counselors need to establish a School-Community Advisory Committee. This Committee should be composed of key stakeholders (e.g., teachers, administrators, parents, students, business and community leaders, and school administrators). This Committee can begin to provide support to your program in order to successfully carry out necessary results-based evaluation activities.

There are many ways to identify the critical issues in your school related to infusing strengths-based career development content into the comprehensive guidance and counseling program (e.g., using needs assessment surveys). For example, targeted focus groups with parents, students, teachers, and business leaders would provide a wealth of ideas about the issues that need to be addressed. It may become apparent that there are problems with the course selection patterns of students in your school (e.g., students not signing up for or passing Advanced Placement courses). Or, it may become evident that students, parents, and teachers are not aware of the great opportunities available in career and technical education coursework in your school. If you hold a career day where students pick someone to job shadow for the day, look to see how many choose to follow a successful entrepreneur. While many young people indicate that they would like to start their own business, most do not have any idea on how to make this happen. These are the kinds of problems that you might find in your school. It is up to you and your research team to identify the critical issues that will lead to greater student success.

D (Describe the problem thoroughly)

Every evaluation activity carried out by a professional school counselor that focuses on a critical problem of practice will have four main components. To remember these, use the mnemonic "SIMS" (Students, Interventions, Measurements, and Settings). In research methodology texts, these issues are discussed under the Construct Validity category (Shadish, Cook, & Campbell, 2002). It is essential that we closely match the operations we are using to the constructs we are aiming to impact. First, we must make sure that the Students involved in our evaluation data collection activities are really representative of the construct we are after. For example, if we want to evaluate a career guidance and counseling intervention for helping at-risk students succeed in school, it is essential that we clearly describe which types of at-risk students participated in our evaluation project and who did not participate. At-risk youth are not a homogenous group. We must be clear about who the students are that we are reporting information on.

Second, we must be very clear that the Intervention we are evaluating is closely tied to the construct we think we are implementing. For example, some of the early studies evaluating which counseling treatments were more effective (e.g., behavioral versus Rogerian, versus psychoanalytic) were confounded when researchers discovered that the behavioral therapists were using more empathy remarks than the Rogerian counselors! If we are evaluating a person-environment fit career intervention and the gains students are making are actually due to enhanced self-efficacy expectations that are being bolstered by this activity rather than to person-environment fit, we would be in danger of confounding the construct validity of our efforts by not clearly understanding what really helps students when they participate in this career intervention.

Third, the Measurements we take must be directly connected to the constructs we intend to investigate. Observations and measurements can be confounded by the influence of unnamed constructs. For example, many studies purport to examine the relationship between academic achievement and race. Upon closer examination however, it becomes apparent that in large part these studies are actually measuring the relationship between academic achievement and socioeconomic status. These studies confound the intended construct of interest by not naming and taking these other (possibly more important) factors into account.

And finally, professional school counselors should be very clear about the Settings in which the intervention takes place. We must be sure we understand the contexts in which an intervention has taken place. For example, suppose you live in a city with a population of approximately 100,000 people. The school district in this city operates about eight elementary schools. Even a casual look at these eight elementary schools will quickly reveal that they are very different from each other. You may find that at least two of the elementary schools have all the strengths and challenges of urban schools. One elementary school is very rural and the others are more typical of suburban schools. These elementary schools are very different places from each other. Even though the state designates the city with only one demographic value, it is quite clear that the community is a very heterogeneous place. A career activity that seems to work in one school setting may not necessarily transfer to other elementary schools that are so markedly different from each other. When results are reported, it is very important that we thoroughly describe contexts and settings within which the activity took place. Interventions clearly need to be tailored to the unique culture and context of each school setting.

By paying close attention to the SIMS (Students, Interventions, Measurements, and Settings), we are in a much better position to make sure that our activities and interventions have fidelity to the constructs that demand attention if students are to succeed. As pointed out by Shadish et al. (2002), such efforts on our part will provide needed attention to make sure that when implementing an activity professional school counselors and teachers have adhered to the instructions, delivered the intervention with fidelity, and that the students have received the treatment in the manner intended. When we can be sure that what we have intended to implement is what is really going on, then we can empower other counselors by providing a clearer blueprint of what needs to take place if the hoped for outcomes for students are to be realized.

E (Use Existing school data)

To say that we live in an age of information is clearly a gross understatement. Like never before in human history, knowledge is accumulating and transforming itself at a breathtaking pace. The Internet and related technologies place this information and expertise at the fingertips of all educational professionals. This is fundamentally an inclusive, democratizing event that creates an opportunity for professional school counselors to fully participate in educational policy debates and school reform initiatives. They can exert influence on the discourse and advocate for the kinds of programs that help all students succeed.

Two points need to be made here. First, schools are inundated with available data on student achievement, performance, and behavior. Schools now routinely disaggregate data to examine differential growth patterns across student groups. Information on the performance of students (e.g., grades, tests scores, attendance, graduation rates, and disciplinary actions) is reported at least at the school building level. Further, most school districts have data management systems to collect, track, and report this data. Usually, there is a person hired to design and manage this system. And second, professional school counselors and other educational professionals who work directly with students do not have the time to mount extensive data collection efforts. In short, data collection should not become another "add on" counselor duty.

Existing school data can be used by professional school counselors and other educational professionals to demonstrate the student growth and development resulting from career guidance and counseling interventions. Professional school counselors can work with the person or persons responsible for managing their district's student data information system to obtain the data they need to evaluate their program. While there are certainly times and occasions when counselors would want to collect data from students that is not routinely collected by their school district, it would be in their best interests to first consider what information is already being collected. Professional school counselors, who become familiar with the school's data system and the people who operate it, could request targeted information needed to answer program evaluation questions. District personnel can easily and routinely place this information into an Excel spreadsheet and send it electronically to the counselor. This is a revolutionary advance and one that graduate training programs should ensure that new counselors know how to fully exploit.

A *(Analyze the data)*

With student data now available in an Excel spreadsheet, how can professional school counselors find meaningful patterns in this existing school data? They need three interrelated sets of skills to be able to find meaningful patterns in the student outcome data they have collected to conduct a results-based evaluation. First, educational professionals should master five basic statistical concepts (i.e., Means, Standard Deviations, Percentages, Correlations, and T-Tests). Second, they need to be able to convert this data into user-friendly tables and figures that clearly communicate results to their audience. And finally, they should be able to conduct qualitative interviews that provide the kind of first hand narrative reports necessary if we are going to understand why an intervention works.

The Big 5. There are five statistical concepts needed to conduct results-based program evaluations. Each is briefly described below. For additional information, any introductory text on statistics would provide more in-depth discussions of each concept.

1. A Mean is a value that tells us something very important about a distribution of scores. It is the average that balances the variability or distances between scores. It is a measure of central tendency that tells us something important about the group of scores as a whole (like the median and mode).

2. A Standard Deviation tells us how large the variability of the scores around the mean is. A Standard Deviation tells us something important about how far scores vary from the mean. Look at any normal curve graph, 68% of all the scores vary within a range of 1 standard deviation above the mean and 1 standard deviation below the mean. Closely related, Z scores tell us how far a score is from the mean in Standard Deviation units. A Z score is like a common denominator that we can use to place different standard deviations on the same scale.

3. Percentages help us to understand that individual scores have meaning only in reference to how everyone else did on a test. Percentages are a way to tell us what the location of someone's score is in relation to all the other scores on the test. It lets us know what percentage of all the people who took the test scored at or below a given score. It makes the meaning of an individual score more meaningful and interpretable. If you are talking to a student who scored at the 95th percentile on a norm referenced test, you would know that this person scored higher than 95% of all the other students taking this test.

4. Correlations help us to understand that if one set of scores varies around the Mean, then two sets of scores can covary with each other. Correlations help us to measure whether or not two sets of scores covary together. Like dancing partners, do these two sets of scores move in rhythm with each other. Do they go up and down together? Or, are they mostly independent from each other so that if I know something about how a student does on one test it tells me nothing about how they are likely to score on a second test? Remember,

we are dealing with patterns that are true for some people some of time. Beware of over-generalizing results to all students in a sample and making erroneous causal claims.

<u>Positive correlation</u>: two scores go up and down together, a positive correlation goes from zero to +1 (e.g., height and weight). On average, taller people tend to weigh more.

<u>Negative correlation</u>: two scores go in opposite directions, as one score goes up the other goes down. A negative correlation goes from zero to -1 (e.g., perfectionism and tolerance for making mistakes). On average, the more perfectionistic a student is the less tolerance they will have for making mistakes.

<u>Non-significant correlation</u>: two sets of scores have nothing to do with each other, they go up or done irrespective of what the other score does (e.g., the last digit on our social security numbers and career satisfaction). On average, the very last digit of our social security numbers has no relationship to how satisfied adults are in their choice of a career.

5. T-Tests help us to test whether the Means of two groups of scores are statistically different from each other. When we want to compare the differences in the performance of two different groups, we can use a T-Test to see if the means of the two groups are statistically different from each other. A T-Test lets us assess whether or not observed differences in the performance of two different groups are statistically significant or due to sampling error.

Once counselors have their student data in an Excel spreadsheet, they can employ user-friendly statistical software to calculate Means, Standard Deviations, Percentages, Correlations, and T-Tests. For example, EZAnalyze (www.ezanalyze.com) was developed by Tim Poynton for professional school counselors. It is freely available for download on the Internet and has excellent tutorials to assist the new user. One of the common complaints about analyzing data in Excel has to do with the difficulty of using the data analysis functions and routines. EZAnalyze solves this problem. The program generates easy to follow, point and click boxes that interface with Excel. In a user-friendly way, EZAnalyze assists counselors to calculate all of the "Big 5" statistics needed for conducting results-based evaluation and many other statistics if the counselor is so inclined. In addition, EZAnalyze easily creates tables and figures out of this data.

Making tables and graphs. This is the situation where a visually appealing picture that clearly communicates the benefits to students who participate in career guidance activities is worth 1,000 words. Professional school counselors are faced with the task of converting their findings into formats that clearly and succinctly communicate to their audience. If they are fortunate enough to gain access to key policy and decision makers, they will likely only have a very short period of time to make their case. When the opportunity presents itself for professional school counselors to talk to parents, administrators, school board members, or elected officials, we need to be armed with a few graphs and tables that succinctly summarize critical outcomes for students who participate in more fully implemented programs.

Table 6-1 presents such a figure. Kuranz and Lapan (2007) reported initial findings for a small group advisory and mentoring program for all 9th graders. This urban high school was very concerned with the high dropout and failure rates for their entering freshmen. It was hoped that a small group advisory experience would help students to feel that they belonged and were wanted in school. The first step to promoting student success was to increase the attendance of 9th graders. During Fall Semester 2004, the guidance small group advisory program was implemented for 9th students.

To evaluate the impact of the small group advisory on student attendance, Kuranz and Lapan used existing school data. To estimate a baseline for 9th graders' attendance patterns, archival data was collected from school records for the 2003-2004 academic year. As reported in Table 6-1, 9th graders in this school had a 94% attendance rate for both the Fall 2003 and Winter 2004 semesters (both girls and boys). However, in Fall Semester 2004 (the first semester that the small group advisory program was in effect) the attendance patterns for all 9th graders increased to 96% (for both girls and boys). Table 6-1 visually depicts this information in a simple, uncomplicated manner.

Two questions are suggested from the data patterns represented in Table 6-1. First, is a 2% increase in attendance an important outcome? And second, why did the attendance go back down to 94% during Winter Semester 2005? The first question can be answered in a number of ways. The 2% gain in attendance for Fall Semester 2004 may or may not be statistically significant. This is not the important question. The importance of this outcome has to be evaluated in its real world context. The school expects 550 9th graders to attend school (that would equal 100% attendance for any one semester). If as was true in the 2003-2004 academic year 94% of these students attend school, that would result in 517 students in attendance for that semester. However, if 96% of the students attend then that would result in 528 students now coming to school. There would be a gain of 11 students who are now attending school, who based on previous year's cohort baseline data we would not expect to come to school. A gain of 11 students is a very important real world outcome.

There are also financial reasons why a 2% increase in student attendance is an important outcome. Kuranz and Lapan estimated that a 2% increase in attendance would earn this financially strapped high school approximately $41,250 more from the state in tuition monies. That is to say, if the school gets $3,750 from the state for each student in attendance then a gain of 11 new students for one semester would earn the high school $41,250 in new revenue. Checking with the school's administration, Kuranz and Lapan found that they had underestimated what the school would gain financially by adding 11 new students to their attendance. The actual dollar value was closer to $45,000. The cost of hiring a new starting Masters-level professional school counselor in this high school is about $40,000 (not including benefits). Therefore, the school has financially gained a few thousand dollars more than it would cost them to hire a new professional school counselor for the entire year.

The second question prompted by a visual inspection of Table 6-1 has to do with why the attendance dropped back down to 94% during Winter Semester 2005. The answer quite simply was that the small group advisory experience was changed from a supportive guidance and counseling encounter to a test preparation experience trying to get students ready for their state's high stakes testing in the Spring of 2005. Reports from teachers, students, counselors, and school administrators all attested to their negative reaction to the change in the small group advisory program.

Table 6-1 provides a clear and succinct picture to aid professional school counselors as they try to get their message across to policymakers. They could make their case in 1 to 2 minutes. They could point to the graph and say three things. First,

Table 6-1

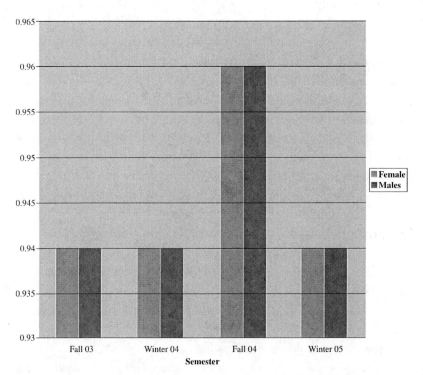

Attendance Patterns for All 9th Graders

a true guidance and counseling small group advisory experience provided to all 9th graders can meaningfully increase student attendance. Second, more students coming to school is a good thing in and of itself. However, it also earns a financially strapped high school needed financial resources. And finally, if professional school counselors are allowed to do work tasks central to the implementation of a comprehensive program then good things can happen for a lot of students. The professional school counselor implementing this program was only able to run this advisory for all 9th graders after the high school principal gave him the time by taking lunch room supervision off of his assigned work tasks (Kuranz & Lapan, 2007). This helps professional school counselors to broach the subject with key decision makers concerning the excessive use of their time on non-guidance tasks that go well beyond "fair share" duties that are shouldered by all educators in a school.

Conducting qualitative evaluation interviews. Shadish et al. (2002) make a compelling case that social science research evaluating the effectiveness of different interventions will only be able to uncover why an intervention works if researchers engage in qualitative evaluation interviews. First hand narrative reports provide an incredibly valuable window to help us see what actually allows an intervention to be successful. In our opinion, professional school counselors have the right skills and training to be highly effective qualitative researchers. They are trained to gather others' perspectives and listen for critical themes that drive the central discourses that shape a school's climate and context. In addition to this orientation, they need the following skills to evaluate their career activities and interventions. They need to be able to do the following four things.

1. Interviews - be able to conduct open-ended and structured interviews
2. Identify Themes - be able to identify critical ideas and themes from interview data
3. Interpretation - interpret the significance of these themes for students, stakeholders, and your program
4. Communication - write out an interpretation of the meaning of your findings in user-friendly ways (e.g., short paragraphs with examples of actual student statements)

Professional school counselors gather this kind of

information, often without even realizing that they are doing it. For example, an urban elementary professional school counselor implemented an anger management program with several students in her school who were exhibiting very problematic aggressive and non-compliant behavior. She gathered both quantitative and qualitative data from her students. Quantitatively, she was able to create several visually compelling graphs that pointed out that there had been a 52% reduction in office visits by these students during the time that the intervention was being implemented. Conservatively translated, this meant that they had saved at least 34 hours of work time for the principal.

She also collected qualitative interview data from the students involved in this program. In her PowerPoint presentation, she followed up the findings from her numbers with brief narrative comments from students. For example, student comments included statements such as:

"More kids play with me at recess now"

"I'm nicer now"

"Maybe I could help other kids with their anger"

These qualitative statements added the personal dimension missing from data on the number of disciplinary referrals. The words of the students really helped to communicate back to the teachers and principal about the far-reaching impact that the intervention had for these young people.

S (Summarize the findings)

Once the data is analyzed, the next step is to Summarize the findings. A PowerPoint presentation can quickly highlight the key findings and effectively communicate to an audience the high quality services that were provided to students. When summarizing your data, it is very important to be clear and concise. An effective PowerPoint presentation would at least contain the following four components.

1. Provide your audience a clear statement of the critical problem that your activity focused on.
2. Briefly describe, in highlights, what you did in response to this problem.
3. In two or three graphs or tables, clearly communicate what you found out.
4. And finally, conclude your PowerPoint by pointing out what you plan in the future to do about this critical problem based on the information you have to help all students and improve your comprehensive program.

! (Use the data to help students)

Now that you have developed an effective PowerPoint presentation it is time to use it to help your students and advocate with policy makers for the resources needed to implement effective programs. The elementary professional school counselor who reduced disciplinary referrals to the principal's office by over 50% developed a very compelling PowerPoint presentation. However, she wasn't going to show it to anyone other than her principal. When asked about the possibility of presenting her findings at a statewide school counseling conference, she deferred and said that she didn't think that she had anything to say. From our perspective, this couldn't be further from the case.

Professional school counselors who implement comprehensive programs make a significant difference in the lives of students and the effectiveness of their schools. By taking the next step and organizing their evaluation efforts using the IDEAS! strategy, they are prepared to enter policy debates and school wide reform initiatives. It is clear that many professional school counselors are making a big difference for their students.

Now, we must move outwards and engage key stakeholders and decision makers. It is not enough to do good work with your students. To garner the support needed to implement effective comprehensive programs, we have to make presentations to our school boards, parent groups, teachers, community leaders, and legislators. Risk using your evaluation results to educate significant others about your role in helping all students succeed. It will benefit your students and help to improve your comprehensive program.

Part Three: Program Audit

This section assists professional school counselors to evaluate the extent to which content from the integrative/contextual model of career development (Lapan, 2004) is being implemented in their schools through their school's comprehensive guidance and counseling program. A step-by-step procedure for doing this is outlined below. Table 6-2 lists the major constructs and components of the integrative/contextual model. Each component is then evaluated on the extent to which the six building blocks of evidence-based practice are used by professional school counselors to promote student growth in each competency area. For example, under the Proactivity, Resilience, and Adaptability construct we want to measure how well each of the six components are being supported by activities that use these six building blocks. We want to know if the comprehensive guidance and counseling program is helping students to develop Direction in their lives by: 1) Building relationships with students; 2) Building support for students at school, home, and in the community; 3) Building connections between students and career role models; 4) Building student understanding of educational and career futures with accurate and up to date information;

5) Building the commitment of students to follow desired paths; and by 6) Building career activities and interventions that are culturally and contextually competent. Take a few minutes to read through and become familiar with Table 6-2.

Table 6-2
Strengths and Evidence-Based Career Guidance Content

Strengths	Six Building Blocks of Evidence-Based Practices					
	Build relationship with students	Build support for students in their immediate environment	Build relationships between students and role models	Build student understanding with accurate and up to date information about postsecondary options and the world of work	Build commitment of students to follow through on decisions and plans	Build culturally and contextually competent activities, interventions, and programs
Proactivity, Resilience, and Adaptability						
1. Direction						
2. Commitment						
3. Preparation						
4. Initiative						
5. Assertiveness						
6. Hopefulness						
Positive Expectations						
1. Self-efficacy for barriers						
2. Self-efficacy for educational requirements and job duties						
3. Outcome expectations						
4. Locus attributions						
5. Stability attributions						
6. Control attributions						

continued on page 179

Table 6-2 (continued)

Identity Developemnt						
1. Specific and clearly defined goals						
2. Difficult and challenging goals						
3. Goals that identify actions to be taken						
4. Career exploration						
5. Meaningful and valued career direction						
6. Self-defined choices						
Understanding yourself and the world of work						
1. Personality orientations						
2. Work values						
3. Abilities, talents, and skills						
4. Interests						
5. Working conditions						
6. Match between self-understanding and the world of work						

continued on page 180

Table 6-2 (continued)

Becoming a successful student and self-regulated lifelong learner					
1. Needed academic skills					
2. Language arts classes					
3. Mathematics classes					
4. Science and technology classes					
5. Interesting academic direction					
6. Self-regulated learner					
Getting along with others					
1. Communication and social skills					
2. Diversity skills and attitudes					
3. Responsible work habits					
4. Positive personal qualities					
5. Emotional balance					
6. Entrepreneurship					
Find and follow your interests and passions					
1. Exploring DATA work tasks					
2. Exploring IDEAS work tasks					
3. Exploring PEOPLE work tasks					
4. Exploring THINGS work tasks					

Step 1: Establish a School-Community Advisory Committee

First, you need to establish a School-Community Advisory Committee that will be able to serve as an "expert panel." This committee will review information that you will present to them on the career guidance and counseling activities offered to students in your school. The members of this Advisory Committee lend legitimacy to your program audit. They are valued community leaders and key stakeholders. They will be the witnesses you need to establish the validity of what you are or are not providing to students. Advisory Committee members would include parents, students, school administrators, school board members, elected officials, business leaders, and community leaders (e.g., clergy or representatives from local child advocacy groups). The School-Community Advisory Committee should include at least six to eight members and be fully informed of their role in this program audit.

Step 2: Assemble program information to present to your School-Community Advisory Committee

Next, gather information on the career guidance and counseling activities that are being implemented in your school. You will be presenting this information to your Advisory Committee. Use the following framework to help you organize this information. Describe interventions from the following perspectives.

A) Title of Intervention.

B) Students: Which students are being served by this intervention (number of students and ages)?

C) Intervention: Briefly describe the intervention, how you deliver it, and how long it takes you to provide this service to students.

D) Measurements: What data are you collecting to evaluate gains for students?

181

    E) Which component of the comprehensive program are you using to deliver this intervention (Guidance Curriculum, Individual Planning, Responsive Services, or Systems Support)?

    F) What outcome data do you have that assesses the benefits for students who participate in this activity?

Step 3: Train School-Community Advisory Committee to use Expert Panel Rating Form

After presenting your information to the Advisory Committee, you want to have them make an overall rating for each box in Table 6-2. For example, you want to know from their perspective how well you are helping students to develop Direction in their lives by Building relationships with them. This is a summative judgment committee so members will make based on the information you will present to them. Every measurement strategy has strengths and weakness, and this one is no exception. Committee members are valued members in your community. Their opinions and perspectives matter a great deal. Their ratings will provide estimates of inter-observer agreement about the level of implementation of the career-related aspects of your comprehensive program. As expert witnesses to what you are doing for students, you will have them make a summative judgment for each box in Table 6-2. Now, train them in how to use the Expert Panel Rating Form so that they can make these judgments.

<u>Expert Panel Rating Form</u>

Please use this scale to rate how accurate each statement is about the implementation of the career development activities and interventions provided to students in your school. This scale is designed to represent a continuum moving on the one end from

"Not at all Accurate" to "Extremely Accurate" on the other end. There is no negative end of the scale. Rather, the purpose of the scale is to provide you an idea of where implementation stands at the present time. You will be provided information about your school on which to base your ratings.

Not at all Accurate		Somewhat Accurate		Very Accurate		Extremely Accurate
1	2	3	4	5	6	7

Now, have each Advisory Committee member make a rating for every box in Table 6-2. For example, their first 6 items that would be rated are:

1. Relationships are built with all students to help them develop Direction in their lives
2. Support is provided to all students in school, at home, and in the community to help them develop Direction in their lives
3. Relationships are established with career role models to help all students develop Direction in their lives
4. Accurate and up to date career-related information is provided to all students to help them develop Direction in their lives
5. Support is provided to help students follow through on educational and career decisions and plans helps students to develop Direction in their lives
6. Culturally and contextually competent career activities are provided to all students to help them develop Direction in their lives

Step 4: Present program information to your School-Community Advisory Committee

Next, take the time to present information on your career guidance and counseling activities to your Advisory Committee. Teach them about what you are doing. Make sure you leave plenty of time for questions and give and take between you and your committee. Make sure they feel comfortable critiquing your work. Instruct them that their role is not be a rubber stamp but to ask tough questions and look for aspects of your program that should be enhanced. They will help you get better and improve your program.

Step 5: Have your School-Community Advisory Committee use the Expert Panel Rating Form to assess program implementation

When you are confident that the Advisory Committee understands your program and how to use the Expert Panel Rating Form, have each committee member fill in every box in Table 6-2. These ratings represent their best assessment of what career guidance and counseling activities are being provided to all students. And, conversely, what is not being provided to students. Again, reassure committee members that you want their honest feedback. The only way to improve services is to accurately examine what is happening for students and what is not being provided.

Step 6: Use EZAnalyze to average your School-Community Advisory Committee members' ratings

Collect Advisory Committee member ratings and enter the data in an Excel spreadsheet. Use EZAnalyze to compute a Mean score for each box in Table 6-2. Do this by averaging the score for each committee member's rating for that box. For example, you would compute a mean for the first box (Relationships are built with all students to help them develop Direction in their lives). This Mean would be the average rating for all committee members related to the implementation of this integrative/contextual model competency in your school. EZAnalyze provides tutorials on how to create and analyze such Excel spreadsheets.

Step 7: Summarize results in PowerPoint presentation

Take the time to identify important patterns and themes in the Mean ratings of the Advisory Committee. Following the IDEAS! suggestions contained in Part 2, develop a PowerPoint presentation that summarizes these results.

Step 8: Present results to your School-Community Advisory Committee

Now, present your findings contained in your PowerPoint to your Advisory Committee. Make sure you take plenty of time to encourage discussion and debate. Provide committee members the opportunity to take issue with your findings or add in additional insights that you may have missed.

Step 9: Incorporate feedback from your School-Community Advisory Committee into PowerPoint presentation

Take the Advisory Committee's feedback and incorporate it into your PowerPoint.

Step 10: Present PowerPoint to school and community leaders

Now, as suggested in the IDEAS! strategy, use the data to improve your program and advocate with policy makers for the resources needed to implement an effective program. Make a presentation to your school board. Make a presentation at your school's Parent Teacher's Association. Visit an elected official and let them know what you are doing. Go to your local Chamber of Commerce and present to business leaders on your career development efforts and what they can do to help you help your students. And don't forget, make sure your school administrators and teachers know about your program!

Part Four: Reflective Practice Exercise

Before you take your School-Community Advisory Committee through this process, take the time now to go through these 10 Steps yourself. This is an opportunity for you to reflect on your practice and assess the areas of strength and areas that need enhancement in your career development activities and interventions. Follow each of the 10 Steps summarized below.

Step 1: You will be the sole rater, as you do not yet have an Advisory Committee.

Step 2: Think about all of the career guidance and counseling activities you currently provide to students.

Step 3: Make sure you know how to use the Expert Panel Rating Form.

Step 4: Think about your career guidance and counseling activities and how they match up with Table 6-2.

Step 5: Use the Expert Panel Rating Form to rate each box in Table 6-2.

Step 6: Enter your data into an Excel spreadsheet. Compute a Mean score for how well you are using each of the 6 Building Blocks of Evidence-Based Practice in your school. Have EZAnalyze generate charts (e.g., a column graph) for your 6 Mean ratings.

Step 7: Summarize your results in a user-friendly PowerPoint presentation. What are the areas of strength and what areas need to be enhanced if you are to help all students develop the educational and career planning skills that they need?

Step 8: Present your results to a friend or colleague.

Step 9: Incorporate your friend or colleague's feedback.

Step 10: Present your improved PowerPoint at a regional or statewide conference for professional school counselors.

A Final Point

This chapter presented strategies professional school counselors can use to carry out a results-based evaluation and conduct an audit of the career guidance and counseling activities currently being provided in their school. Professional school counselors assess the extent to which strengths-based career services are provided to all students through comprehensive guidance and counseling programs. Evaluation is a win/win situation for professional school counselors. Students win when the services provided to them are consistently improved. Professional school counselors win when they are able to demonstrate to key policy makers that what they do benefits all students. Conducting a results-based evaluation is an opportunity professional school counselors should eagerly embrace.

References

Garner, R. (1990). When children and adults do not use learning strategies: Toward a theory of settings. *Review of Educational Research, 60*(4), 517-529.

Gysbers, N. C., & Henderson, P. (2006). *Developing & managing your school guidance and counseling program.* Alexandria, VA: American Counseling Association.

Herr, E. L., & Cramer, S. H. (1972). *Vocational guidance and career development in the schools: Toward a systems approach.* Boston: Houghton Mifflin.

Kuranz, M. H., & Lapan, R. T. (2007, July). *School counselor and counselor educator research collaboration.* Presented at the annual convention of the American School Counselor Association, Denver, CO.

Lapan, R. T. (2004). *Career development across K-16 years: Connecting the present to satisfying and successful futures.* Alexandria, VA: American Counseling Association.

Lapan, R. T. (2005, December). *Training school counselors to do results-based evaluation.* Presented as a pre-conference workshop for the Association for Career and Technical Education, Kansas City, MO.

Shadish, W. R., Cook, T. D., & Campbell, D. T. (2002). *Experimental and quasi-experimental designs for causal inference.* Boston: Houghton Mifflin Company.

Slavin, R. (2002, April). Keynote address presented at the annual conference of the American Educational Research Association, New Orleans, LA.

Chapter 7

Advocating for Strengths-Based Career Development Through Comprehensive Guidance and Counseling Programs

- "I can hardly wait to get to school each day because I know I will learn something that is important to me. Teachers and counselors link their subjects and programs to my strengths, skill, talents, interests and dreams, and try to make sure that I feel competent, confident and connected. I always feel successful at the end of the day."

- "I have an education/career plan that keeps me focused and helps me make connections between what I am learning in school and success in the adult world. Because of this, I always know what I am learning, why I am learning it, and how I will be able to use it when I am no longer in school. I review and adjust my plan regularly."

- "I have assumed major responsibility for my academic progress, and am regularly setting, assessing and adjusting my educational and career goals." (Crow, 2006a)

Strengths-Based Career Development for School Guidance and Counseling Programs

Imagine a school where students make statements such as these about their education and its importance to them. Students who make these statements feel connected to school because their experiences in school are meaningful to them. They have found purpose and direction for and connection to their education and their current and possible future lives.

What happens when students find purpose, direction, and connection? The research evidence indicates that they do better academically, are more likely to be fully engaged in the classroom, and have improved attendance. In addition, they are less likely to exhibit descriptive behavior, school violence, substance abuse, and emotional stress (Wingspread Declaration on School Connections, 2004). When students are connected to school they believe "that adults [advocates] in school care about their learning as well as about them as individuals" (p. 233).

A major goal for professional school counselors, teachers, and other educational personnel, working within the framework of comprehensive guidance programs is to help all students connect to school by being their advocates (Ratts, DeKruyf, & Chen-Hayes, 2007). This means helping all students find purpose and direction in their education and their future lives. Career guidance and counseling content and activities drawn from the career domain and the related domains of academic and personal/social, infused with strengths-based career development content, play central roles in helping all students succeed in school and plan for the future.

What is advocacy? Advocacy is "the act of pleading for, supporting or recommending: active espousal" (*Random House Webster's Unabridged Dictionary*, 2001, p. 30). Who is an advocate? An advocate is an individual "who speaks or writes in support or defense of a person or cause" (p. 30).

Based on these definitions, what are the required

advocacy roles and competencies for professional school counselors and other educational personnel as they work to help all students succeed in school and plan for their possible futures? Lewis, Arnold, House, and Toporek (2005) developed an Advocacy Competency Domains model as shown in Figure 7-1 that outlines advocacy roles and responsibilities. The model identifies advocacy competencies in working directly with students, in working within the school of the district, and in working with the public concerning public awareness about the importance of career guidance and counseling in the schools as well as social/political advocacy at state and national levels.

Figure 7-1

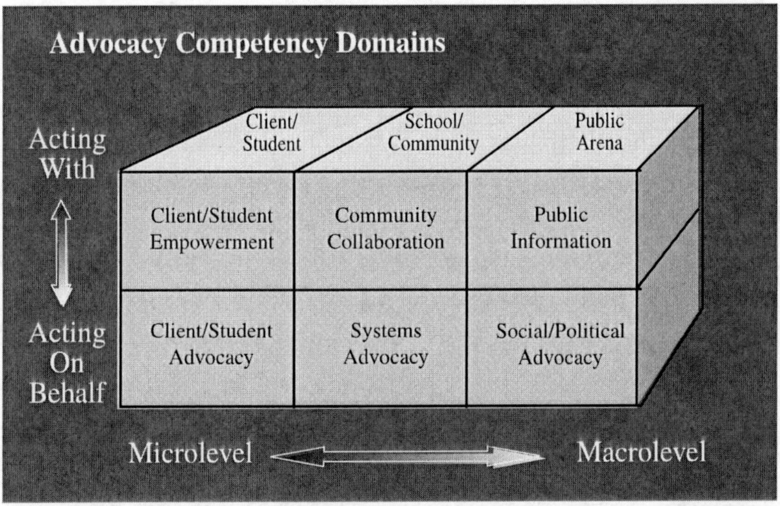

Advocacy Competency Domains

	Client/Student	School/Community	Public Arena
Acting With ↑↓	Client/Student Empowerment	Community Collaboration	Public Information
Acting On Behalf	Client/Student Advocacy	Systems Advocacy	Social/Political Advocacy

Microlevel ⟷ Macrolevel

Note: From *Advocacy competency domains,* by J. Lewis, M. Arnold, R. House, and R. Toporek, 2005, Alexandria, VA: American Counseling Association. Reprinted with permission.

Using the model's three fold approach to advocacy, Chapter 7 opens by focusing on professional school counselors' advocacy work with students and their parents or guardians, providing students with support and encouragement helping them connect to and become fully engaged in school (Bemak & Chung, 2005). It does so by highlighting professional school counselors' ethical responsibilities to be student advocates. Professional school counselors are actively involved advocates for students and comprehensive guidance and counseling programs that feature career guidance and counseling activities. "The advocate… can develop high aspirations rather than just attending to aspirations as they emerge" (Stone, 2004, p. 28). Specific standards from the ASCA Ethical Standards for School Counselors (2004) are reviewed that highlight professional school counselor student advocacy responsibilities for career guidance and counseling.

Next, Chapter 7 focuses on professional school counselors' advocacy roles and responsibilities to work inside the schools of the district on behalf of students. This means working toward the goal of fully implemented comprehensive guidance and counseling programs that feature career guidance and counseling activities and services for all students K-12. This means working toward the goal of all professional school counselors in the district working full-time within the framework of the program.

Chapter 7 then describes the important professional school counselors' advocacy roles and responsibilities concerning public awareness and social/political advocacy. First, specific attention is given to informing the public about the importance of career guidance and counseling within the framework of comprehensive guidance and counseling programs. Second, the importance of social/political advocacy at the state and national levels is stressed, particularly the importance of state and national legislation for career guidance and counseling as part of overall guidance and counseling programming.

Ethical Responsibilities for Student Advocacy

In the Preamble of the American School Counselor Association's *Ethical Standards for School Counselors* (2004), it states that professional school counselors are advocates. Note the following words:

Professional school counselors are advocates, leaders, collaborators, and consultants who create opportunities for equity in access and success in educational opportunities by connecting their programs to the mission of schools and subscribing to the following tenets of professional responsibility:

• Each person has the right to be respected, be treated with dignity and have access to a comprehensive school counseling program that advocates for and affirms all students from diverse populations regardless of ethnic/racial status, age, economic status, special needs, English as a second language or other language group, immigration status, sexual orientation, gender, gender identity/expression, family types, religious/spiritual identity and appearance.

• Each person has the right to receive the information and support needed to move toward self-direction and self-development and affirmation within one's group identities, with special care being given to students who have historically not received adequate educational services: students of color, low socio-economic students, students with disabilities and students with nondominant language backgrounds.

- Each person has the right to understand the full magnitude and meaning of his/her educational choices and how those choices will affect future opportunities.

The first point in the Ethical Standards highlights the fact that all students of all circumstances, backgrounds, and conditions have the right to access comprehensive guidance and counseling programs. The second point emphasizes that all students have the right to receive information and support while the third point stresses that all students have the right to understand their choices now and in the future. All three statements focus on the "rights" of students to have access to guidance and counseling programs, receive information and support, and understand their choices.

Notice the emphasis on career guidance and counseling in these statements, particularly statement three with its focus on students understanding the impact of their choices. Notice also that these statements do not say it would be "nice" for these things to happen. These statements say students have "rights" to these things; they are "rights" that are due to students as delineated in the Ethical Standards. Strong words indeed!

In the main text of the *Ethical Standards for School Counselors* (ASCA, 2004), specific advocacy responsibilities for professional school counselors are identified in five sections: A.1. Responsibilities to Students, A.3. Counseling Plans, B.1. Parent Rights and Responsibilities, D.1. Responsibilities to the School, and D.2. Responsibility to the Community, as follows:

A.1. Responsibilities to Students

The Professional school counselor:

　　b. Is concerned with the educational, academic, career, and personal/social needs and encourages the maximum development of every student.

A.3. Counseling Plans

The Professional school counselor:

a. Provides students with a comprehensive school counseling program that includes a strong emphasis on working jointly with all students to develop academic and career goals.

b. Advocates for counseling plans supporting student's right to choose from the wide array of options when they leave secondary education. Such plans will be regularly reviewed to update students regarding critical information they need to make informed decisions.

B.1. Parent Rights and Responsibilities

The Professional school counselor:

a. Respects the rights and responsibilities of parents/guardians for their children and endeavors to establish, as appropriate, a collaborative relationship with parents/guardians to facilitate the student's maximum development.

D.1. Responsibilities to the School

The Professional school counselor:

c. Is knowledgeable and supportive of the school's mission and connects his/her program to the school's mission.

D.2. Responsibility to the Community.

The Professional school counselor:

b. Extends his/her influence and opportunity to deliver a comprehensive school counseling program to all students by collaborating with community resources for student success.

It is clear from the *Ethical Standards for School Counselors* (ASCA, 2004) that professional school counselors have ethical responsibilities to be advocates for students, responsibilities that are required. Notice also how many times student advocacy is tied directly to career guidance and counseling. The focus is on educational choices and future opportunities; meeting educational, academic, career, and personal/social student needs; the development of academic and career goals; choosing from a wide array of options; and on making informed decisions.

Because advocacy is embedded in the *Ethical Standards for School Counselors* (ASCA, 2004), professional school counselors are required to be advocates acting on behalf of students. These are the standards to which courts of law hold school counselors accountable. They are the imperatives of the profession.

Given the ethical imperatives to be student advocates, what must professional school counselors do? First and foremost, it is important to engage students in their education so that they feel competent, confident, and connected. Marks (as cited in Klem & Connell, 2004) conceptualized engagement as:

A psychological process, specifically the attention, interest, investment, and effort students expend in the work of learning." She also offered definitions of other researchers including: "students' involvement with school, [a sense of belonging and an acceptance of the goals of schooling]"; their "psychological investment in and effort directed toward learning, understanding, or mastering the knowledge, skills, or crafts that academic work is intended to promote" and students' "interest" and "emotional involvement" with school, including their "motivation to learn." (p. 262)

Notice the words Marks used as well as those she quoted from other researchers to describe the essence of engagement, words such as attention, interest, investment, involvement, belonging, emotional involvement, and motivation to learn. Think about the meaning of these words in the context of student advocacy. Think about how the meaning of these words can be operationalized by professional school counselors and other educators within the framework of comprehensive guidance and counseling programs that emphasize career guidance and counseling activities infused with strengths-based career development content.

Pellitteri, Stern, Shelton, and Muller-Ackerman (2006) suggested that emotional factors and emotional intelligence strongly influences academic success. They also highlighted the importance of emotional intelligence in career development.

> . . . career development involves deeply personal self-examination and complex decision-making processes. Using emotions in an intelligent manner is important in making career choices. (p. 6)

To put these concepts into action, Crow (2006b) suggested that professional school counselors and teachers, working within the framework of comprehensive guidance and counseling programs, should focus on outcomes that will facilitate student engagement. What are some example outcomes? Crow identified 14 possible outcomes he thought professional school counselors and teachers should focus on to help students become fully engaged in school (see Table 7-1).

Given the ethical imperative that professional school counselors are student advocates, what knowledge, skills, and attitudes are required? Trusty and Brown (2005) presented a list of advocacy competencies grouped under the categories of dispositions, knowledge, and skills. Under each they described in detail what professional school counselors should know and be able to do. They emphasized that advocacy dispositions are foundational to advocacy knowledge and skills. "If school counselors do not have advocacy dispositions, it will not be

Table 7-1

Student Engagement Outcomes

In their work with students, school counselors and teachers should help students:

1. Understand and appreciate who they are, where they are going, and how they can get there. Included here are learning styles/modalities and multiple intelligences.
2. Identify, develop, and maximize their strengths, skills, talents, and potential.
3. Engage from their "hearts and souls" as well as from their heads.
4. Operate at the three highest levels of cognition on Bloom's Taxonomy.
5. Always describe 1) what they are learning, 2) why they are learning it, and 3) how they can use it (the difference it will make in their lives).
6. Describe their dreams and to visualize paths for realizing them.
7. Develop learner, worker, and success identities.
8. Feel competent, confident, and connected.
9. Develop a decision-making process that they understand and can articulate.
10. Develop a "sense of planfulness."
11. Have education/career/success plans and be able to describe them whenever asked.
12. Have an understanding of the world they will be entering when they leave school.
13. Become independent and self-sufficient.
14. Become more resilient and increase their sense of self-efficacy.

Note: From "Possible Elements of a Comprehensive Guidance and Counseling Program" by C. Crow, 2006. Used with permission.

possible to develop skills" (p. 261). Trusty and Brown (2005) also developed a model of advocacy for professional school counselors. They suggested that the following steps are important in any advocacy efforts:

- Develop advocacy dispositions
- Develop advocacy relationships and advocacy knowledge
- Define the advocacy problem
- Develop action plans
- Implement action plans
- Make an evaluation
- Celebrate or regroup (p. 264)

The Advocacy Model (see Figure 7-1) developed by Lewis, Arnold, House, and Toporek (2005) describes advocacy competencies as having two dimensions; one acting with students to empower them and one acting on behalf of students to advocate for them. When working with students, professional school counselors use the direct interventions of the guidance curriculum, individual student planning, and responsive services featuring career guidance and counseling. When acting on behalf of students, professional school counselors help remove barriers to students' career, academic, and personal/social development.

Program Advocacy Within Schools

As work continues to fully implement comprehensive guidance and counseling programs that feature career guidance and counseling, attention to program advocacy is a requirement. Program advocacy and fully implemented programs go hand-in-hand. Program advocacy supports and encourages fully implemented programs. Fully implemented programs provide data to support and encourage program advocacy.

What is within schools advocacy? It involves professional

school counselors and school counseling leaders speaking with teachers, parents, administrators, and other educational personnel about the need for and importance of fully implemented comprehensive guidance and counseling programs that focus on career guidance and counseling. It means working with local boards of education to develop local school district policies for guidance and counseling.

A Fully Implemented Program

Within school program advocacy is critical to the successful implementation of comprehensive guidance and counseling programs. The best local advocacy strategy is a strong, vital, and fully implemented program that contributes directly to overall student success including academic achievement. When a fully implemented program is delivering career guidance and counseling and the related academic and personal/social activities and services to all students, the program is visible, and hence is informing those involved about its importance in the educational system. A fully implemented comprehensive guidance and counseling program is student advocacy in action.

School Board Policies

Another within program advocacy strategy is to make sure there is an appropriate school board policy for guidance and counseling including career guidance and counseling. What is a policy? According to *Random House Webster's Unabridged Dictionary* (2001), a policy is "a course of action adopted and pursued by a government.... "

What is the status of policies that govern comprehensive guidance and counseling programs at the local level? Gysbers, Lapan, and Jones (2000) found that local policies for guidance and counseling had not kept pace with the program approach to guidance and counseling. Most still followed the traditional position/services model.

What policy for guidance and counseling exists in your school district? Work with your administration to review what exists and then help write a new policy or update an old policy. In it, highlight the importance of career guidance and counseling as an important part of the districts' comprehensive guidance and counseling program. When written appropriately and then adopted by the board of education, such a policy is advocacy at work.

Local Program Activities

Local program advocacy also involves developing a variety of advocacy resources including local websites, flyers, and PowerPoint presentations that describe comprehensive guidance and counseling programs including career guidance and counseling, all showing results data. It involves active and involved professional school counselors using these resources to talk with individuals and groups in and out of school. School board presentations are particularly important.

Career guidance and counseling activities are particularly well suited for advocacy work. For example, individual student education and career plans focus on helping students take rigorous course work and carefully plan their futures. Parents or guardians and students are involved in regular meetings with professional school counselors or other educators to review these plans. In addition, career days/nights and post secondary planning days/nights are also highly visible career guidance and counseling activities that feature student advocacy because the goals of these activities are to extend and expand students' opportunities. If students don't know about opportunities, they cannot take advantage of them. Opportunities unknown are not opportunities at all.

Public Awareness

Unfortunately, the work of professional school counselors is still misunderstood and, as a result, is often undervalued by the public. The public remains uninformed about the importance of fully implemented comprehensive guidance and counseling programs that feature career guidance and counseling and the related academic and personal/social activities, and services for all students. They often don't understand why such programs and the work of professional school counselors are critical for student success.

School-Community Advisory Committee

One way to communicate clearly and directly with the public is to form and use a school-community advisory committee for the district's comprehensive guidance and counseling program. It is composed of representatives for the school and community. The membership of this committee will vary according to the size of the school district and the community and can include such individuals as an administrator (assistant superintendent, principal); the guidance program leader; a representative of the teaching staff; a representative from the mental health community; a representative from the parent-teacher association; and a newspaper editor or other media representative.

The school-community advisory committee acts as a liaison between the school and community and provides recommendations concerning the needs of students and the community. A primary duty of the committee is to advise those involved in the guidance program improvement effort. The committee is not a policy- or decision-making body; rather it is a source of advice, counsel, and support. It is a communication link between those involved in the guidance program improvement effort and the school and community. The use and involvement of a school-community advisory committee will vary according to the program and the community, but in all cases membership must be more than in name only. Community involvement and interaction are important, and advisory committee members can be particularly helpful in developing and implementing the public relations plans for the community.

A Public Advocacy Plan

As stated previously, the best local advocacy strategy is a strong, vital, and fully implemented guidance and counseling program that features career guidance and counseling and related academic and personal/social activities and services. It is a success story waiting to be told, but telling it requires a plan. In establishing an advocacy plan, consider the following points:

1. Establish goals for your public advocacy plan. Examples include the public being informed about, understanding of, and being supportive of the program.
2. Identifying the public populations that need to be reached.
3. Find out what these publics know about and think about the program and what they think the program should be delivering to all students.
4. Develop the resources needed to operationalize the advocacy plan using local, national, and state school counselor materials and events.
   - National School Counselor Week
   - PowerPoint presentations
   - Program flyers and pamphlets
   - PTA newsletters
   - School district newsletters
   - Websites
5. Establish the time lines for public advocacy work remembering that public advocacy is ongoing, it is not a one time event.

Social/Political Advocacy at State and National Levels

Social/Political advocacy means working with the state boards of education and state legislators to write state education rules and legislation supporting comprehensive guidance and counseling programs. It means working with national legislators to support comprehensive guidance and counseling through national legislation. It means using the authority and resources of the American School Counselor Association and its state divisions.

State Program Advocacy

Some progress has been made in program advocacy at the state level with the passage of state legislation or state board of education rules. For example, the state of Utah has a state rule for comprehensive guidance (Utah State Board of Education Rule for Comprehensive Guidance, 2008). In this rule, specific attention is given to career guidance and counseling within comprehensive guidance programs by emphasizing that all students are required to develop and use Student Education and Occupation Plans (SOEP) beginning in grade seven.

The state of Texas passed a law in 2001 titled "An Act Relating to Public School Counselors, S.B. 518". In it, school counselors are required to work with school faculty and staff, students, parents, and the community to plan, implement, and evaluate developmental guidance and counseling programs. In these programs, there shall be a guidance curriculum to help students develop their full educational potential including the students' interests and career objectives. In addition there shall be an individual planning system to guide students as they plan, monitor, and manage their educational, career, and personal/social development. Notice how career guidance and counseling are featured within this legislation promoting comprehensive guidance and counseling programs.

In 2006, the state of Washington passed a state law focusing on comprehensive guidance programs. Section one of the law stated:

> The legislature recognizes that there are specific skills and a body of knowledge that each student needs to chart a course through middle school, high school, and post-high school options. Each student needs active involvement from parents and at least one supportive adult in the school who knows the student well and cares about the student's progress and future. Students, parents, and teachers also need the benefit of immediate feedback and accurate diagnosis of students' academic strengths and weaknesses to inform the students' short-term and long-term plans. To empower and motivate all students and parents to take a greater role in charting the students' own educational experiences, the legislature intends to strengthen schools' guidance and planning programs. (Improving Student Performance through Student-Centered Planning, 2006)

Note the focus of Washington's state law. It is on helping students gain the knowledge and skills needed to plan their education and future lives, the main goal of career guidance and counseling.

National Program Advocacy

A major step forward in national advocacy was taken by

the American School Counselor Association (ASCA) with the introduction of *The ASCA National Model: A Framework for School Counseling Programs* (2003). By publishing the National Model, ASCA raised the level of awareness and visibility of comprehensive guidance and counseling programs in general and career guidance and counseling specifically. Comprehensive guidance and counseling programs and career guidance and counseling are now beginning to be included in national discussions about educational reform (Association for Career and Technical Education, n.d.). However, much advocacy work remains since many recent national publications focusing on educational reform do not mention guidance and counseling as being part of the solution (National Center on Education and the Economy, 2007).

Substantial work is needed concerning advocacy for comprehensive guidance and counseling including career guidance and counseling in national legislation. For example, the Carl D. Perkins Career and Technical Education Improvement Act of 2006 is defined in Section 3. Definitions as follows:

(7) Career Guidance and Academic Counseling—The term 'career guidance and academic counseling' means guidance and counseling that –

(A) provides access for students (and parents, as appropriate) to information regarding career awareness and planning with respect to an individuals' occupational and academic future; and
(B) provides information with respect to career options, financial aid, and postsecondary options, including baccalaureate degree programs.

At the same time, later in Section 118c of this Act, career guidance and academic counseling are described as being "programs designed to promote career and education decision making by students (and parents, as appropriate) regarding education (including postsecondary education) and training options and preparations for high skill, high wage, or high demand occupations and non-traditional fields."

The question is, is the language of this Carl D. Perkins Act sufficient to adequately describe comprehensive guidance and counseling programs that feature career guidance and counseling? In Section 3, note that the focus is on providing information. In Section 118 however, career guidance and academic counseling is described as a program focusing on decision making. The answer to the question is no, these definitions are not sufficient. Much work is needed at the national policy level to help all to understand the contributions of comprehensive guidance and counseling programs that emphasize career guidance and counseling.

There is much advocacy work to do at the national level. Working with legislators and their staffs at the national level is extremely important. The Guidance and Career Development Division of the Association for Career and Technical Education is one vehicle to impact national legislation, particularly the language for career guidance and counseling in any forthcoming revisions of the current Carl D. Perkins Career and Technical Education Improvement Act of 2006. The American School Counselor Association and the American Counseling Association are also active in promoting legislation for guidance and counseling in the schools. Advocacy materials from the American Counseling Association such as the document "Effective Advocacy and Communication with Legislators" (American Counseling Association, 2006) are particularly useful.

Summing Up

Advocacy for students and comprehensive guidance and counseling programs that feature career guidance and counseling cannot be an afterthought or something that would be nice to do, but is not considered as necessary. Advocacy is an ethical responsibility that requires our full attention throughout all phases of program development, implementation, and enhancement. Advocacy begins when comprehensive guidance and counseling programs are being planned and designed or are being updated and revitalized and continues unabated. Advocacy is never over!

References

American Counseling Association. (2006). *Effective advocacy and communication with legislators.* Alexandria, VA: Author.

American School Counselor Association (ASCA). (2004). *Ethical standards for school counselors.* Alexandria, VA: Author.

American School Counselor Association. (2003). *The ASCA national model: A framework for school counseling programs.* Alexandria, VA: Author.

An Act Relating to Public School Counselors, SB 518, Amends Texas Education Code, Sections 33.001, 33.005-33.006 (2001).

Association for Career and Technical education (n.d.). *The role of the guidance profession in a shifting education system.* Alexandria, VA: Author.

Bemak, F., & Chung, R. C. (2005). Advocacy as a critical role for urban school counselors: Working toward equity and social justice. *Professional School Counseling, 8,* 196-202.

Carl D. Perkins Career and Technical Education Improvement Act of 2006, 109th Congress, 1st session, S 250 (2006).

Crow, C. (2006a, August). *Comprehensive guidance and counseling: A deeper look.* Paper handout presented at the Oregon Department of Education's Comprehensive Guidance and Counseling Implementation Training for School Counselors, Teachers, and Administrators, Cohorts A, B, and C. Portland, OR.

Crow, C. (2006b, August). *Possible elements of a comprehensive guidance and counseling program.* Paper handout presented at the Oregon Department of Education's Comprehensive Guidance and Counseling Implementation Training for School Counselors, Teachers, and Administrators, Cohorts A, B, and C. Portland, OR.

Gysbers, N. C., Lapan, R. T., and Jones, B. (2000). School board policies for guidance and counseling: A call to action. *Professional School Counseling, 3*, 349-353.

Improving student performance through student-centered planning, ESSB 6255, (2006).

Klem, A. M., & Connell, J. P. (2004). Relationships matter: Linking teacher support to student engagement and achievement. *Journal of School Health, 74*, 262-273.

National Center on Education and the Economy. (2007). *Executive summary. Tough choices tough times. The report of the new commission on the skills of the American workforce.* Washington, DC: Author.

Lewis, J., Arnold, M., House, R., & Toporek, R. (2005). *Advocacy competencies.* Alexandria, VA: American Counseling Association. Retrieved January 2, 2007, from http://www.counseling.org/Resources/

Pellitteri, J., Stern, R., Shelton, C., & Muller-Ackerman, B. (2006). *Emotionally intelligent school counseling.* Mahwah, NJ: Lawrence Erlbaum Associates.

Random House Webster's Unabridged Dictionary (2nd ed.). (2001). New York: Random House.

Ratts, M. J., DeKruyf, L., & Chen-Hayes, S. F. (2007). The ACA advocacy competencies: A social justice advocacy framework for professional school counselors. *Professional School Counseling, 11*, 90-97.

Stone, C. B. (2004). Hands-on high tech advocacy. *ASCA School Counselor, 41*, 23-38.

Trusty, J., & Brown, D. (2005). Advocacy competencies for professional school counselors. *Professional School Counseling, 8*, 259-265.

Utah State Board of Education Rule for *Comprehensive Guidance Programs*, R277-462-3 (2008).

Wingspread declaration on school connections. (2004). *Journal of School Health, 74*, 233-234.

Epilogue

Taking the Next Steps:
Putting Your Knowledge and Skills to Work

By now you have finished the last chapter of the book on Advocacy and may be wondering about what you can do to become an advocate and develop and implement a comprehensive guidance and counseling program that features strengths-based career development. What steps do you need to take? We recommend using the five steps of planning, designing, implementing, evaluating, and enhancing (Gysbers & Henderson, 2006).

Step One: Planning

The first phase of Planning is called "Getting Organized to Get There From Where You Are." It involves identifying and understanding the necessary conditions for change in your school building and district. Are the individuals involved ready for change? Will some individuals resist? Is there sufficient trust among school counselors, teachers, and administrators? In this first phase, a presentation to the administration and the district board of education that describes needed improvements in the district's existing comprehensive guidance and counseling program is important. The second phase of planning is called "Conducting a

Thorough Assessment of Your Current Program." The purpose of the thorough assessment of your current program is to determine the degree to which the program is in place in your school and/or district. This is important because a comprehensive program is the best vehicle to deliver strengths-based career development activities to all students. The American School Counselor Association's National Model (2005) has a program audit form that can be used for this purpose. The state of Missouri also has developed an audit process called the Internal Improvement Review (IIR) that can be used for this purpose. A copy of the IIR is available at the Missouri Center for Career Education web site, http://mcce.org.

Another purpose is to conduct an assessment of student needs as seen by students, parents, teachers, administrators, and school counselors. What knowledge and skills do students require to be successful in school, in post-secondary education, at work, and in life. Data from this assessment can be used to guide the selection and placement of strengths-based career development activities within the guidance curriculum and individual student planning program components.

Step Two: Designing

The major task in designing is to put your full, complete, desired comprehensive guidance and counseling program on paper. The comprehensive program described in Chapter 3, Figure 3-1, provides a framework to use for this purpose. Writing the program on paper doesn't mean the program will be implemented automatically. However, without writing the program down first, there is no structure and organization to implement.

In using Figure 3-1 in Chapter 3, begin with the Content Element. What strengths-based career development content should be emphasized in the program? The assessment of student needs data collected in Step One can help establish content priorities when coupled with the judgment of school counselors and teachers. It will help identify strengths-based career development content and the related content from the academic and personal-social domains by school levels, by grade level groupings, or by grade levels.

Continue using Figure 3-1 to put your program on paper. Focus on the Organizational Framework Element next and write your program definition, choose and write down the assumptions you are making about your program and the students and parents being served, and write down your program rationale. Then move to the Program Components.

Lay out on paper the guidance curriculum featuring strengths-based career development content and the related content form the academic and personal-social domains by grade levels decided upon using the needs assessment data and the judgments of school counselors and teachers. Select the units to be used and organize a calendar showing when and where the units will be taught to ensure schools will master the guidance and counseling content they require.

Next describe on paper the individual student planning process you will use. Describe the form you will be using giving it an appropriate name such as "a personal plan of study," "a life career plan," or a "learning plan." Then describe the processes you will be using beginning in middle school to help students, working closely with parents, to develop, monitor, and manage their plans middle school through high school. Remember that student participation in guidance curriculum activities is foundational to the individual planning process.

The written description of Responsive Services is next. Descriptions of individual counseling and small group counseling topics should be listed. Consultation should be defined and the topics and people to be consulted should be listed. Finally, the referral process and referral sources should also be described and listed.

Next, all of the activities in the System Support Component need to be identified and described briefly. See Figure 3-1 in Chapter 3 for a list of possible activities to include in System Support. Remember that all of the activities in the System Support Component are legitimate guidance and counseling support activities. No non-guidance tasks are to be listed since they are outside of the program.

Finally, in the writing down process, it is necessary to consider possible allocations of school counselor time. In Figure 3-1 in Chapter 3, note the suggested time allocations. These time allocations are suggested as points to consider. Once the program is underway, time allocations may change.

Step Three: Implementing

By the end of the design process, the full program should have been written and be ready for implementation. The task now is to fully implement the program. This involves calendaring the program across grade levels as well as allocating school counselor time. It also involves working closely with teachers helping them integrate strengths-based career development content into their curricula. In addition, it involves making sure the individual student planning component is put into operation beginning at the middle school level.

Implementing the comprehensive program with its strengths-based career development focus requires time and energy to overcome possible implementation barriers. What barriers may need to be overcome? They include "the weight of tradition," resistance to change," and "the burden of non-counseling tasks."

Overcoming Tradition

Tradition is a strong force to overcome, and yet, schools must overcome it to fully implement comprehensive guidance and counseling programs. In overcoming tradition in school counseling, the goal is not to discard the good work that has been done and is being done by school counselors operating in the traditional position-services mode. The goal is to embed this approach within the organizational framework of K-12 programs to enable all school counselors to think and plan collectively so they can work more effectively in their buildings. By embedding the position approach and services model within comprehensive programs, school counselors can be converted from professionals with lists of duties to professionals who have total comprehensive guidance and counseling programs to develop and implement, providing services to all students and their parents systematically and sequentially K-12. When this is done, school counselors will no longer be seen as office people; they will be seen as program people.

Reckon with Change

Change is inevitable. Too often schools and districts treat implementing comprehensive school counseling programs as a one-time event. They generate enthusiasm about implementing the programs, hold events to launch the programs, but then, the challenge of everyday events smothers any follow-through implementation procedures. We are good at holding "first annuals" but often find it difficult to complete the full implementation process. Make no mistake; program implementation is a process, not an event. Districts must build sufficient time and resources into the implementation process if they plan to attain full implementation.

Districts must also take into account the magnitude of the change process, shifting from the traditional position approach and services model to a comprehensive program approach. Some individuals view change as simply an extension of what exists. Others see change as a substantial shift from what exists. The problem occurs when one group sees change as simply an extension of the past and consistent with current values, whereas another group sees the same change as a substantial break from the past that conflicts with current values. It is important to find out how the individuals involved in change view it. Is the change needed to fully implement comprehensive school counseling programs seen as an extension of what is by school counselors, but a substantial change or break from the past by administrators? Or vice versa? It makes a difference and will affect whether the implementation process occurs smoothly, unevenly or not at all.

Focus on Time-on-Task

Writing down the program is the first step in implementing it. Having a written program doesn't mean the program is automatically implemented, but you can't implement something that isn't there. A key to implementing the written program is calendaring. Calendaring requires you to lay out planned program activities and services over the four component areas—guidance curriculum, individual student planning, responsive services, and system support—throughout the course of the year. Pay careful attention to time-on-task in this process so at least 80 percent of school counselor time is spent in direct services to students and parents (guidance curriculum, individual student planning, and responsive services) and 20 percent or less is spent in indirect services (system support). The time given to various program components varies by grade level and is reviewed periodically and modified according to student and building needs.

Full implementation of comprehensive school counseling programs requires school counselors to spend 100 percent of their time providing activities and services to all students and their parents as well as to teaches and administrators. One hundred percent school counselor time-on-task means administration must reassign the non-school –counseling-related tasks many school counselors currently perform. Remember these inappropriate tasks are ones that are above and beyond the fair-share tasks all school counselors carry out as members of a school district's faculty.

Closing the Implementation Gap

Closing the implementation gap is not an end in itself. Closing the gap is a means to an end. The end is a fully implemented comprehensive school counseling program that provides school counselors and other personnel who work in the program with the time-on-task, content, structure, resources, and data to assist all students to connect firmly and positively to school.

Step Four: Evaluating

The task in evaluating the program is to follow the formula, program+personnel=results. The first part of this task is to once again review your comprehensive program to see if it is fully implemented. The audit procedures described in Step One can be used once again to see if the program is functioning fully. The second part of the task is to evaluate the work of the personnel in the program using appropriate performance-based forms and procedures. If you go to the Missouri Center for Career Education web site (http://mcce.org), you will find a narrated PowerPoint presentation that describes this process. The third part of this task is to evaluate the results of the program. Chapter 6 of the book provides specific instructions concerning evaluating the results of the program.

Step Five: Enhancing

After gathering program, personnel, and results evaluation data for several years, it is time to step back and rethink your entire program. It is time to consider redesigning the program to incorporate any smaller revisions you have been making on a regular basis. Also, enough time has probably elapsed from the time you gathered student, school, and community data to the time you designed your original program, that student needs and school and community circumstances have changed. This redesign process is called program enhancement.

Redesigning is based not only on conclusions drawn through evaluation but also on learning from the passage of time in implementing your comprehensive guidance and counseling program as well as on new realities that are currently present in your district and community. Redesigning the program periodically is how you ensure its relevancy for your students and the program's content, clients, and activities. It may also lead to new or shifted priorities for the use of school counselors' time and talent.

It is important to remember that the redesign process does not change the basic framework of the program. The framework of the program found in the structural components and program components remains the same. What will change is the content of the program, the descriptions and assumptions of the program, the activities and services provided in the program, and the use of school counselor time and talent. Program and personnel priorities also will change.

What steps are involved in the program redesign process? Gysbers and Henderson (2006) suggested that you use the same steps that were used in the original process of program development (planning, designing, implementing, evaluating, and enhancing) as you redesign your existing program. The program enhancement process is done periodically following evaluation and connects back to the beginning as the program redesign process unfolds. Each time this is done the program improves. Thus the process is spiral, not circular. Each time the redesign unfolds, a new and more effective comprehensive guidance and counseling program emerges.

Concluding Thoughts

As you are taking the necessary steps to put your knowledge and skills to work, keep in mind the following three points described by Gysbers and Henderson in their book *Developing and Managing Your School Guidance and Counseling Program* (2006, p. x).

Ongoing Program Improvement

Some readers may think that guidance and counseling program improvement is a simple task requiring little staff time and few resources. This is not true. Substantial work can be completed during the first several years, but at least 4 to 5 years with the necessary resources available to ensure successful implementation are usually required. To carry the program through the enhancement phase may require an additional 5 years. Then an ongoing program improvement process is recommended.

Common Language

It is important to understand that a comprehensive guidance and counseling program provides common language for the program elements that enable students, parents, teachers, administrators, school board members, and school counselors in a school district to speak with a common voice when they describe what a program is. They all see the same thing and use the same language to describe the program's framework. This is the power of common language whether the program is in a small or large, rural or urban or suburban school district.

Flexibility and Opportunity

Within the basic common language framework at the local district level, however, the guidance knowledge and skills (competencies) students are to learn, the activities and services to be provided, and the allocations of school counselor time are tailored specifically to student, school, and community needs and local resources. This provides the flexibility and opportunity for creativity for the personnel in every school district to develop and implement a comprehensive guidance and counseling program that makes sense for their districts.

References

American School Counselor Association. (2005). *The ASCA National Model: A framework for school counseling programs* (2nd ed.). Alexandria, VA: Author.

Gysbers, N. C., & Henderson, P. (2006). *Developing and managing your school guidance and counseling program* (4th ed.). Alexandria, VA: American Counseling Association.

Appendix

A Career Guidance and Counseling Unit for Grade 7

How Do the Pieces Fit?

Note: From the Missouri Comprehensive Guidance Programs, Missouri Department of Elementary and Secondary Education. Retrieved November 11, 2008, from http://missouricareereducation.org/curr/cmd/guidanceplacementG/lessons/careerms.php. Used with permission.

Strengths-Based Career Development for School Guidance and Counseling Programs

Unit # 1 Title: How Do the Pieces Fit?   **Grade Level: 7**

Number of Lessons in Unit: 3

Time Required: Usually 50 minutes; however, length will vary depending on the length of the inventories selected.

Best time of year to implement this Unit: Anytime

Lesson Titles:
Lesson 1: If the Career Fits, Explore It!
> Materials/Special Preparation Required:
>> A Career interest inventory: Your local school district, most likely, has adopted an interest inventory. Review the inventory's purpose, district's use of inventory and relevance/application to 7th grader's exploration of their interests. If the district has not adopted a specific inventory, explore interest inventories available free via the internet and commercial sources. Examples of interest inventories include: Job-O, Career Game, COIN Career Targets, Kuder, CX Bridges Career Explorer, Choices

Lesson 2: If the Career Fits, Explore It! (Part 2)
> Materials/Special Preparation Required:
>> Completed career interest inventory (See Lesson 1)
>> Career information resources: Print (e.g., *Occupational Outlook Handbook*) and electronic
>> Activity Sheets: "Who I Am..." "Researching a Career" (optional

Lesson 3: We Are All Pieces of the Puzzle
> Materials/Special Preparation Required:
>> Completed "Who I Am ..." and "Researching a Career" Activity Sheets (see Lesson 2)
>> Activity Sheet: "Map It Out" concept map (2 copies for each student)
>> Item(s) purchased locally and produced in another country

Missouri Comprehensive Guidance Standard:
CD.7: Applying Career Exploration and Planning Skills in the Achievement of Life Career Goals.
CD.8: Knowing Where and How to Obtain Information About the World of Work and Post-Secondary Training/Education.

Grade Level Expectation:
CD.7.A.07.a.i: Use current interests, strengths, and limitations to guide career exploration and educational planning.
CD.7.B.07.a.i: Be aware of occupations and careers as they relate to career paths and personal interests/aptitudes.
CD.7.C.07.a.i: Recognize the relevance of all work and workers and that they coexist in a global society.

CD.8.A.07.a.i: Utilize career and educational information to explore career paths of interest.
CD.8.B.07.a.i: Utilize a variety of resources to obtain information about the levels of training
and education required for various occupations.

American School Counselor Association National Standard (ASCA):
Career Development
- A: Students will acquire the skills to investigate the world of work in relation to knowledge of self and to make informed career decisions.
- C: Students will understand the relationship between personal qualities, education, training and the world of work.

Show Me Standards: Performance Goals (check one or more that apply)

	Goal 1: gather, analyze and apply information and ideas
X	2. Conduct research to answer questions and evaluate information and ideas.
	6. Discover and evaluate written, visual and oral presentations and works.
	8. Organize data, information and ideas into useful forms (including charts, graphs, outlines) for analysis.
	Goal 2: communicate effectively within and beyond the classroom
X	1. Plan and make written, oral and visual presentations for a variety of purposes and audiences.
	Goal 3: recognize and solve problems
	Goal 4: make decisions and act as responsible members of society
X	1. Explain reasoning and identify information used to support decisions.
	8. Explore, prepare for and seek educational and job opportunities.

This lesson supports the development of skills in the following academic content areas.

Academic Content Area(s)		Specific Skill(s)
X	Communication Arts	Reading and writing; compare and contrast; research
X	Mathematics	Data analysis
X	Social Studies	Understanding the value of individuals in a global society
	Science	
	Health/Physical Education	
	Fine Arts	

Lesson Assessment (acceptable evidence):
Career interest inventory, such as Job-O, Career Game, COIN Career Targets, Kuder, CX Bridges Career Explorer, Choices, etc., and authentic assessment through inclusion in career portfolio.
Data on careers and the training required.
Question answer, group discussion, group task completion.

Missouri Comprehensive Guidance Programs: Linking School Success to Life Success
To ensure that the work of educators participating in this project will be available for the use of schools, the Department of Elementary
and Secondary Education grants permission for the use of this material for non-commercial purposes only.

223

Strengths-Based Career Development for School Guidance and Counseling Programs

Brief Summary of Unit: Students will identify personal strengths and interests through use of an interest inventory. They will evaluate the relationship between their preconceived ideas about work with information from a research project. They will also categorize the career with the appropriate career path.

When presented with a product, students will brainstorm the occupations that contribute to the production of that product, classifying the various careers according to the Career Paths.

Unit Goals: Students will complete an interest inventory; use the information from the inventory to investigate careers using written or computerized resources; create and present a career project incorporating personal interests; categorize an occupation based on the Career Paths model.

Students will investigate and/or brainstorm various careers/products to recognize the relevance of all workers and that they coexist in a global society.

Students' Prior Knowledge:

Student success in any learning endeavor is dependent upon prior knowledge. The Missouri Comprehensive Guidance Program Curriculum builds on each student's prior knowledge and understanding in academic content as well as Comprehensive Guidance content. Helping students develop a common vocabulary and common conceptual understandings rests upon the Professional School Counselor.

For the Career Development Strand the common vocabulary for seventh graders includes:

Work	Job Responsibilities of Workers	College, University
Career	Interests	Strength,
Limitation		
Career Paths	Post-secondary Options	Ethics
Resume	Portfolio	Interview

For CD 7 the common conceptual understanding includes: the integration of self knowledge into life and career plans, adapting to changes in the world economy and work, respect for all work (and workers)

For CD 8 the common conceptual understanding includes: the career decision-making processes and the education and training requirements of careers.

At the seventh grade level, students are expected to have prior knowledge of:

The Concept and Titles of the Career Paths	Basic Goal-Setting and Planning Skills
The Importance of All Work	The Value of All Workers
Basic Interviewing Skills	Their Personal Characteristics

Appendix

Unit # 1 Title: How Do the Pieces Fit?

Lesson Title: If the Career Fits, Explore It! (Part 1)   **Lesson**: 1 of 3

Grade Level: 7

Length of Lesson: one class period

Missouri Comprehensive Guidance Standard:
CD.7: Applying Career Exploration and Planning Skills in the Achievement of Life Career Goals.
CD.8: Knowing Where and How to Obtain Information About the World of Work and Post-Secondary Training/Education.

Grade Level Expectation (GLE):
CD.7.A.07.a.i: Use current interests, strengths, and limitations to guide career exploration and educational planning.
CD.7.B.07.a.i: Be aware of occupations and careers as they relate to career paths and personal interests/aptitudes.
CD.8.A.07.a.i: Utilize career and educational information to explore career paths of interest.
CD.8.B.07.a.i: Utilize a variety of resources to obtain information about the levels of training and education required for various occupations.

American School Counselor Association National Standard (ASCA):
Career Development
   A: Students will acquire the skills to investigate the world of work in relation to knowledge of self and to make informed career decisions.
   C: Students will understand the relationship between personal qualities, education, training and the world of work.

Materials (include activity sheets and/ or supporting resources)
A Career interest inventory: Your local school district, most likely, has adopted an interest inventory. Review the inventory's purpose, district's use of inventory and relevance/application to 7th grader's exploration of their interests. If the district has not adopted a specific inventory, explore interest inventories available free via the internet and commercial sources. Examples of interest inventories include: Job-O, Career Game, COIN Career Targets, Kuder, CX Bridges Career Explorer, Choices

Show Me Standards: Performance Goals (check one or more that apply)

	Goal 1: gather, analyze and apply information and ideas
X	2. Conduct research to answer questions and evaluate information and ideas.
	6. Discover and evaluate written, visual and oral presentations and works.
	Goal 2: communicate effectively within and beyond the classroom
	Goal 3: recognize and solve problems
X	Goal 4: make decisions and act as responsible members of society
	1. Explain reasoning and identify information used to support decisions.

Missouri Comprehensive Guidance Programs: Linking School Success to Life Success
To ensure that the work of educators participating in this project will be available for the use of schools, the Department of Elementary and Secondary Education grants permission for the use of this material for non-commercial purposes only.

225

Strengths-Based Career Development for School Guidance and Counseling Programs

8.	Explore, prepare for and seek educational and job opportunities.

This lesson supports the development of skills in the following academic content areas.

Academic Content Area(s)		Specific Skill(s)
X	Communication Arts	Reading and writing; compare and contrast; research
X	Mathematics	Data analysis
	Social Studies	
	Science	
	Health/Physical Education	
	Fine Arts	

Enduring Life Skill(s)

	Perseverance		Integrity	X	Problem Solving
X	Courage		Compassion		Tolerance
	Respect	X	Goal Setting		

Lesson Assessment (acceptable evidence):

Assessment should relate to the performance outcome for goals, objectives and GLE's. Assessment can be question answer, performance activity, etc.
Career interest inventory, such as those listed above, and authentic assessment through inclusion in career portfolio

Lesson Preparation

Essential Questions: How does *who you are* relate to possible choices for careers and career paths? How would an interest inventory help someone have an understanding of oneself?

Engagement (Hook): Partners tell each other qualities they see in one another and what career(s) they think they might be good at.

Procedures for Session 1

Instructor Procedures:	Student Involvement:
1. Introduce the Interest Inventory. Emphasize the intended purpose of interest inventories (to compare their interests with the interests of workers in specific occupations), how the inventory was developed AND to whom students' interests were compared to yield the students' results (people in the "norming" group). Stress the importance of sincere and deliberate responding. Administer the career interest inventory.	1. Ask clarifying questions about the inventory. Complete the career interest inventory thoughtfully and deliberately.
2. When the inventory has been completed, allow time for students to talk about their thinking as they were completing it, e.g.,	2. Post-inventory: Reflect on process and respond to questions

Missouri Comprehensive Guidance Programs: Linking School Success to Life Success

To ensure that the work of educators participating in this project will be available for the use of schools, the Department of Elementary and Secondary Education grants permission for the use of this material for non-commercial purposes only.

226

Did they "just do it" or did they do it thoughtfully and with a curiosity about themselves and their results? Help students anticipate their results as a way to gain interesting information to consider when making decisions about careers. (NOTE: It is important that EVERY student develops an awareness of his or her interests as measured by a comprehensive inventory; thus, plan a separate session for those who may have difficulty completing the inventory in a large group setting).	
3. Tell students that the results of the inventory will be used in the next lesson (Unit 1 Lesson 2). When using an online interest inventory, print a copy of each student's results.	3. Students will share closing comments.

Teacher Follow-Up Activities

Students post their name in the correct area of a career path chart. Names are followed by one or two strengths the student possesses that attracted them to their correct path.

Counselor reflection notes (completed after the lesson)

Strengths-Based Career Development for School Guidance and Counseling Programs

Unit # 1 Title: How Do the Pieces Fit?

Lesson Title: If the Career Fits, Explore It! (Part 2)   **Lesson:** 2 of 3

Grade Level: 7

Length of Lesson: 50 minutes

Missouri Comprehensive Guidance Standard:
CD.7: Applying Career Exploration and Planning Skills in the Achievement of Life Career Goals.
CD.8: Knowing Where and How to Obtain Information About the World of Work and Post-Secondary Training/Education.

Grade Level Expectations (GLEs):
CD.7.A.07.a.i: Use current interests, strengths, and limitations to guide career exploration and educational planning.
CD.7.B.07.a.i: Be aware of occupations and careers as they relate to career paths and personal interests/aptitudes.
CD.8.A.07.a.i: Utilize career and educational information to explore career paths of interest.
CD.8.B.07.a.i: Utilize a variety of resources to obtain information about the levels of training and education required for various occupations.

American School Counselor Association National Standard (ASCA):
Career Development
A: Students will acquire the skills to investigate the world of work in relation to knowledge of self and to make informed career decisions.
C: Students will understand the relationship between personal qualities, education, training and the world of work.

Materials (include activity sheets and/ or supporting resources)
Completed career interest inventory (See Lesson 1)
Career information resources: Print (e.g., *Occupational Outlook Handbook*) and electronic
Activity Sheets: "Who I Am…" "Researching a Career" (optional)

Show Me Standards: Performance Goals (check one or more that apply)

	Goal 1: gather, analyze and apply information and ideas
	2. Conduct research to answer questions and evaluate information and ideas.
X	6. Discover and evaluate written, visual and oral presentations and works.
	Goal 2: communicate effectively within and beyond the classroom
	Goal 3: recognize and solve problems
	Goal 4: make decisions and act as responsible members of society
X	1. Explain reasoning and identify information used to support decisions.
	8. Explore, prepare for and seek educational and job opportunities.

Missouri Comprehensive Guidance Programs: Linking School Success to Life Success
To ensure that the work of educators participating in this project will be available for the use of schools, the Department of Elementary
and Secondary Education grants permission for the use of this material for non-commercial purposes only.

228

Appendix

This lesson supports the development of skills in the following academic content areas.

Academic Content Area(s)		Specific Skill(s)
X	Communication Arts	Reading and writing; compare and contrast; research
X	Mathematics	Data analysis
	Social Studies	
X	Science	Scientific inquiry
	Health/Physical Education	
	Fine Arts	

Enduring Life Skill(s)

	Perseverance		Integrity	X	Problem Solving
X	Courage		Compassion		Tolerance
	Respect	X	Goal Setting		

Lesson Assessment (acceptable evidence):

**Assessment should relate to the performance outcome for goals, objectives and GLE's.
Assessment can be question answer, performance activity, etc.**
Question answer, group discussion, group task completion

Lesson Preparation

Essential Questions: How does who I am relate to Career Paths and career choices?

Engagement (Hook): TOMORROW'S THE DAY!!!

Procedures:

Instructor Procedures:	Student Involvement:
1. Say to students: You HAVE to get a job by noon TOMORROW!! The magic is … You have the ability get the job of your dreams … a job that will allow you to BE YOURSELF!! What will it be? You will use that job as you review the results of the interest inventory you completed during the last guidance lesson.	1. Students will identify a job.
2. Return students' career interest inventory results. Allow time for the students to review the information. Stress the limitations of individual results: • Are your results "YOU"? • How do your results fit with the job you identified in #1? • The person who "takes" an interest inventory MUST USE the results (NOT let the results USE THEM) with information	2. Students will review and reflect HONESTLY on their individual results and consider the results in relation to the job identified above. They will ask clarifying questions.

Strengths-Based Career Development for School Guidance and Counseling Programs

CD7-8-Gr7-Unit1-Lesson2.doc Page 3 of 7
Created by S. Wymore, L. Bunch, G. Tipton

they know to be true about themselves (e.g., "The truth is, I made a design when I darkened the bubbles—and have no idea what the question asked.").	
3. Review Career Paths and the attributes of those individuals who work in each. Compare the results of their interest inventories, the careers in each Career Path and the job they identified in "1" above. Is there a fit? Would you still choose the job you chose in #1? Would you like to take the interest inventory again?	3. Students will engage in a comparison of the career paths, workers, and the results of the interest inventories …in light of the job they identified in "1" above.
4. Provide instructions for the "Who I Am…" Activity Sheet and have students complete it by marking an X in the boxes that are "like them". *NOTE: Students may be unfamiliar with the vocabulary on this Activity Sheet. The counselor may choose to read the items and offer explanation as questions arise.*	4. Review the "Who I Am …" Activity Sheet and ask clarifying questions.
5. Collect the completed Activity Sheets. Tell students that during the next guidance lesson, they will be using the results and that between now and then, they will be discovering more about a specific occupation."	5. Complete Step 1 of "Who I Am…" Activity Sheet; give to counselor when complete.
6. Explain that students are to research at least three occupations that are in the areas of high interest for them. Encourage students to investigate any career titles that are not familiar to them. Using one or more resources, students will research three careers of interest. From those three options, students will choose one that they will address when doing their reality check. While students are investigating a specific career, they should consider which Career Path that occupation "fits".	6. Students will research three possible careers based on career inventory results, choosing one that they will focus on for further investigation. Students will use highlighters to mark information about the career they have chosen, such as salary, working conditions, location, tasks and responsibilities, working alone or with others. (During the next guidance lesson, they will be using the information gained from their career research to complete Step 2 of "Who I Am…."

7. Help students explore the career information resources available to them – on the internet, in the counselor's office, in the school library.	7. Students may use information downloaded from an online source OR if they are unable to print a hard copy of their career information from an online source, they can use the Activity Sheet "Researching a Job" to record information they find during the research they conduct.

Teacher Follow-Up Activities

Students post careers they investigated on a classroom career path chart.

Counselor reflection notes (completed after the lesson)

Missouri Comprehensive Guidance Programs:　　　　　　Linking School Success to Life Success
To ensure that the work of educators participating in this project will be available for the use of schools, the Department of Elementary
and Secondary Education grants permission for the use of this material for non-commercial purposes only.

Strengths-Based Career Development for School Guidance and Counseling Programs

Activity Sheet: Researching a Career

Name: _____ Grade: _____

Career: _____

Career Path: _____

Average salary/wage: _____ Hours/work days: _____

Describe work and working conditions:

_____
_____
_____
_____
_____
_____
_____
_____

High school courses that will help you prepare for this job:

_____
_____
_____
_____
_____
_____
_____
_____

Education or training needed beyond high school to prepare you for this job:

_____
_____
_____
_____
_____
_____

Missouri Comprehensive Guidance Programs: Linking School Success to Life Success
To ensure that the work of educators participating in this project will be available for the use of schools, the Department of Elementary and Secondary Education grants permission for the use of this material for non-commercial purposes only.

232

Appendix

Activity Sheet: Who I Am ....

Name: _____ **Grade:** _____

A Career I'm Considering: _____

Career Path: _____

Step 1 Directions: Place an X in front of the statements that reflect your interests, abilities, and talents.

☐ High salary (over $50,000)	☐ Working in a wet place	☐ Working in a safe place
☐ Middle income ($20,000 to $50,000)	☐ Working in some hazardous surroundings	☐ Working at the same location all day
☐ Low income (under $20,000)	☐ Pleasant working conditions	☐ Working inside
☐ Staying clean	☐ Working outside	☐ Getting dirty
☐ Working in a factory	☐ Working in a rural setting	☐ Working in many areas
☐ Working in a store	☐ Working in an office	☐ Traveling as part of the job
☐ Working in a noisy place	☐ Working with other people	☐ Working in a quiet place
☐ Working in heat	☐ Planning your own work	☐ Working alone
☐ Working in cold	☐ Doing work that provides a chance to be creative	☐ Working in air conditioning
☐ Working in a dry place	☐ Doing the same task each day	☐ Having a high level of responsibility
☐ Following orders	☐ Spending lots of time with your family	☐ Doing different tasks every day
☐ Working a seasonal job	☐ Being your own boss	☐ Having vacation time
☐ Working for someone else	☐ Working short hours	☐ Having flexible hours
☐ Performing mental, rather than physical, tasks	☐ Working a regular 40-hour week	☐ Having respect in the community
☐ Working with details	☐ Working with tools	☐ Performing physical, rather than mental, tasks

Missouri Comprehensive Guidance Programs: Linking School Success to Life Success

Strengths-Based Career Development for School Guidance and Counseling Programs

☐ Having good fringe benefits	☐ Manufacturing a product	☐ Performing a service
☐ Working while standing	☐ Working while sitting	☐ Helping people
☐ Doing work that requires a great deal of reading and writing	☐ Competing with others	☐ Working in an expanding career area
☐ Motivating others	☐ Influencing others	☐ Working in a city
☐ Working in the suburbs	☐ Supervising others	☐ Making decisions on the job
☐ Working in a declining career area	☐ No high school diploma or GED required	☐ Social skills required
☐ Listening skills required	☐ Following directions carefully	☐ Trade or technical school required
☐ Working with a chance for advancement	☐ Advanced college degree required	☐ Using writing skills
☐ Using speaking skills	☐ Using reading skills	☐ On-the-job training required
☐ Apprenticeship offered	☐ License required	☐ Memory skills required
☐ Working as a member of a team	☐ Good grooming required	☐ Using science skills
☐ Advanced math skills required	☐ Basic math skills required	☐ Union membership required
☐ Typing skills required	☐ Special skills required	☐ College degree required
☐ Social studies skills required	☐ Good manners required	☐ Working by myself

Step 2 Directions: Place an O in front of the statements that are true for the career you researched.

Look closely at your responses. If there are both X's and O's in front of each of the statements, the career you are considering should appeal to you. If many of the X's (true for YOU) and O's (true for the career you researched) are not beside the same statements, you may need to rethink your reasons for considering this career as a potential career choice.

Unit # 1 Title: How Do the Pieces Fit?

Lesson Title: We Are All Pieces of the Puzzle   **Lesson:** 3 of 3

Grade Level: 7

Length of Lesson: 30 minutes

Missouri Comprehensive Guidance Standard:
CD.7: Applying Career Exploration and Planning Skills in the Achievement of Life Career Goals.
CD.8: Knowing Where and How to Obtain Information About the World of Work and Post-Secondary Training/Education.

Grade Level Expectation (GLE):
CD.7.C.07.a.i: Recognize the relevance of all work and workers and that they coexist in a global society.

American School Counselor Association National Standard (ASCA):
Career Development
  A: Students will acquire the skills to investigate the world of work in relation to knowledge of self and to make informed career decisions.
  C: Students will understand the relationship between personal qualities, education, training and the world of work.

Materials (include activity sheets and/ or supporting resources)
Completed "Who I Am ..." and "Researching a Career" Activity Sheets (see Lesson 2)
Activity Sheet: "Map It Out" concept map (2 copies for each student);
Item(s) purchased locally and produced in another country

Show Me Standards: Performance Goals (check one or more that apply)

	Goal 1: gather, analyze and apply information and ideas
X	6. Discover and evaluate patterns and relationships in information, ideas and structures.
	8. Organize data, information and ideas into useful forms (including charts, graphs, outlines) for analysis.
	Goal 2: communicate effectively within and beyond the classroom
X	1. Plan and make written, oral and visual presentations for a variety of purposes and audiences.
	Goal 3: recognize and solve problems
	Goal 4: make decisions and act as responsible members of society
X	1. Explain reasoning and identify information used to support decisions.
	8. Explore, prepare for and seek educational and job opportunities.

Missouri Comprehensive Guidance Programs: Linking School Success to Life Success
To ensure that the work of educators participating in this project will be available for the use of schools, the Department of Elementary
and Secondary Education grants permission for the use of this material for non-commercial purposes only.

235

Strengths-Based Career Development for School Guidance and Counseling Programs

This lesson supports the development of skills in the following academic content areas.

	Academic Content Area(s)	Specific Skill(s)
X	Communication Arts	Expressing ideas verbally; compare and contrast
	Mathematics	
X	Social Studies	Understanding the value of individuals in a global society
	Science	
	Health/Physical Education	
	Fine Arts	

Enduring Life Skill(s)

	Perseverance	X	Integrity	X	Problem Solving
X	Courage		Compassion	X	Tolerance
X	Respect		Goal Setting		

Lesson Assessment (acceptable evidence):

Assessment should relate to the performance outcome for goals, objectives and GLE's. Assessment can be question answer, performance activity, portfolio, etc.
Students will be able to use mapping skills related to careers and career paths.

Lesson Preparation

Essential Questions:
How are various occupations interrelated? How do those occupations relate to the career paths?

Engagement (Hook):
Show students a small puzzle. Explain that without all the pieces, a puzzle is not complete. The same principle applies to the world of work. Each person who provides a service or who produces a product depends on others to make the process complete.

Procedures for Lesson

Instructor Procedures:	Student Involvement:
1. Distribute students' completed "Who I Am ..." Activity Sheets. Have them complete the second part of the inventory: With one of the careers they researched in mind, students will mark the items that "fit" that career with an "0"	1. Students will complete the second part of the Activity Sheet and review the "match" asking himself or herself if their preferences would make them a good fit with the occupation they researched.
2. Divide students into task groups. Give each group a "Map It Out" concept map Activity Sheet. Encourage the groups to choose a specific career that they find appealing. The students will write the name of that career in the middle bubble.	2. Participate in group discussion while respecting the views of others.

Appendix

Ask the groups to consider related careers. Related careers are those that may not be the specific career goal, but would allow students to be professionally involved in the career area desired. With every specific career, there are typically many related careers. The students will then brainstorm as many related careers as possible, placing them in the Career Path boxes. Encourage the students to come up with as many jobs in as many Career Paths as possible. Some jobs may have many Career Paths involved. Others may not.
Example: A specific career may be a news anchor-person. Related careers might include camera operator, copywriter, free-lance writer, reporter, producer, actor, and sportscaster.

Allow 5 minutes for students to complete the concept map.

3. Review the groups' results, soliciting opinions from the rest of the class.

3. When concept map is complete, groups will explain their choices for related occupations either to the whole class group or to another small task group.

4. Present items purchased in the United States and produced in another country to the groups. Have them consider all the potential individuals who may have contributed to that product being available for purchase in the local store. Give the groups another copy of the "Map It Out" Activity Sheet to use for this activity; telling students to place the name of the product in the center and the names of occupations in the career path "boxes" surrounding the product. Allow 5 minutes for students to complete the concept map.

4. Review group roles and ways of showing disagreement without being disagreeable. Consider the many people who have work because of this product--in the country of origin and in the United States. Students will contribute ideas and listen to others' ideas through brainstorming, group discussion, and class discussion.

5. Discuss the results of the groups' concept mapping exercise. Follow up with discussion of a global society, the value of all work and workers and the

5. Students will do a 2-minute writing as closure. The focus will be: "My piece of the puzzle ...". Entries will be included in the students' Personal Plan of

Missouri Comprehensive Guidance Programs: Linking School Success to Life Success
To ensure that the work of educators participating in this project will be available for the use of schools, the Department of Elementary and Secondary Education grants permission for the use of this material for non-commercial purposes only.

237

Strengths-Based Career Development for School Guidance and Counseling Programs

CD7-8-Gr7-Unit1-Lesson3.doc Page 4 of 5
Created by S. Wymore, L. Bunch, G.Tiption

interdependence of people all over the world.	Study/Career Portfolio.

Teacher Follow-Up Activities

Teacher may want to post Activity Sheets on bulletin board so students can visually understand many examples of how various careers are dependent on one another.

Counselor reflection notes (completed after the lesson)

Missouri Comprehensive Guidance Programs: Linking School Success to Life Success
To ensure that the work of educators participating in this project will be available for the use of schools, the Department of Elementary and Secondary Education grants permission for the use of this material for non-commercial purposes only.

238

CD7-8-Gr7-Unit1-Lesson3.doc Page 5 of 5
Created by S. Wymore, L. Bunch, G.Tiption

Activity Sheet: Map It Out!

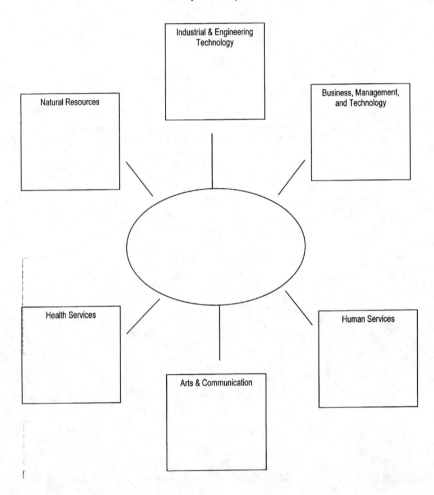